BRITISH FRIGATE
vs
FRENCH FRIGATE

1793–1814

MARK LARDAS

First published in Great Britain in 2013 by Osprey Publishing,
Midland House, West Way, Botley, Oxford, OX2 0PH, UK
43-01 21st Street, Suite 220B, Long Island City, NY 11101
E-mail: info@ospreypublishing.com

Osprey Publishing is part of the Osprey Group

A CIP catalogue record for this book is available from the British Library

Print ISBN 978 1 78096 132 3
PDF ebook ISBN: 978 1 78096 133 0
ePub ebook ISBN: 978 1 78096 134 7

Index by Zoe Ross
Typeset in ITC Conduit and Adobe Garamond
Maps by bounford.com
Originated by PDQ Media, Bungay, UK
Printed in China through Asia Pacific Offset Limited.

13 14 15 16 17   10 9 8 7 6 5 4 3 2 1

Osprey Publishing is supporting the Woodland Trust, the UK's leading
woodland conservation charity, by funding the dedication of trees.

www.ospreypublishing.com

Author's acknowledgements

Thanks go to the Houston Maritime Museum and its dedicated staff.
University of Houston–Clear Lake's Neumann Library was an invaluable
source of material on this book and many others that I have done over the
years. A mention also needs to go to Rama Neko, who provided me with both
images related to and sources about the *Marine nationale*.

Author's note

The following abbreviations indicate the sources of the illustrations used
in this volume:

AC – Author's Collection
AP-HMM – Author photo taken in the Houston Maritime Museum
LOC – Library of Congress, Washington, DC
Rama – Photograph by Rama Neko, Wikimedia Commons, Cc-by-sa-2.0-fr
Rama-PD - Public domain image provided by Rama Neko
USNA – United States Naval Academy

Other sources are listed in full.

Author's dedication

This book is dedicated to my son Nicholas, who helps develop today's airborne
equivalent of the scouting sailing frigate.

Editor's note

For ease of comparison please refer to the following conversion table:

1 nautical mile = 1.9km
1yd = 0.9m
1ft = 0.3m
1in = 2.54cm/25.4mm
1 ton (UK) = 1.016 metric tonnes
1lb = 0.45kg
1 fathom = 6ft/1.8m

Artist's note

Readers may care to note that the original paintings from which the cover
and battlescenes of this book were prepared are available for private sale. All
reproduction copyright whatsoever is retained by the Publishers. All enquiries
should be addressed to:

Peter Dennis, 'Fieldhead', The Park, Mansfield, Nottinghamshire NG18 2AT,
UK, or email magie.h@ntlworld.com

The Publishers regret that they can enter into no correspondence upon
this matter.

CONTENTS

INTRODUCTION

To command a sailing frigate – whether in Britain's Royal Navy or France's *Marine nationale* – was a glorious thing. Frigate commands were prized. Fast and well armed, they were said to be able to beat anything they could catch, and out-sail anything they could not beat. While they served with the navies' battle fleets, they were rarely chained to the line of battle. Rather, they were the eyes of the fleet, scouting ahead in search of the enemy fleet.

They also served as commerce raiders, seeking out enemy merchantmen, waiting to sweep in like a wolf seizing a sheep. Alternatively, they escorted convoys, dutiful sheepdogs protecting their merchant flock from privateers or naval warships, the other wolves of the sea. Or they could be dispatched on diplomatic or exploration missions to the far corners of the world – expeditions important enough to require a fast, powerful ship, but not worth weakening the line-of-battle by detaching a ship-of-the-line from the fleet.

To command a frigate was to have independence, a rare privilege for all but the most senior naval officers. Even when frigates were assigned to three- to six-ship cruiser squadrons, frigate captains were expected to act independently, to seize opportunities when they appeared, and not to wait for direction from the senior captain. Moreover, there were never enough frigates. (Horatio Nelson was reputed to have written, 'Was I to die this moment, "Want of Frigates" would be found stamped on my heart.') Frigates frequently had to be sent individually on independent missions, or as the lead ship in a collection of lesser sloops-of-war.

As a result, frigate captains, generally on the lower half of the captains' list, often had more autonomy and responsibility than the more senior captains at the top of the list. Those senior captains, commanding larger, more powerful ships-of-the-line, were usually tied to a fleet, in the line of battle and under the thumb of the admiral commanding.

Ships-of-the-line rarely saw battle outside of a fleet action, and fleet actions were rare. During the period covered by this book, 1793 to 1814, France and Britain fought only around a dozen fleet actions, and none after 1806. Frigates were frequently in combat. Some actions were as simple as firing a shot over the bow of a merchant vessel to compel surrender. But frigates fought hundreds of actions against privateers, participated in scores of skirmishes or battles between frigate squadrons, and fought dozens of single-ship actions.

HMS *Belle Poule* chasing a privateer. Taken from France in 1780, *Belle Poule* served as a frigate in the Royal Navy throughout much of the period covered by this book before being converted to a troop ship in 1814. (AC)

Not all of the single-ship actions fought between 1793, when France and Britain declared war in the wake of the French Revolution, and 1814, when Napoleon abdicated and accepted exile at Elba, were fought between frigates. Most the single-ship actions were unequal fights: a frigate catching a smaller sloop-of-war or corvette or a frigate getting trapped by a ship-of-the-line. (Despite the myth that a frigate could run from anything it could not fight, given the right wind conditions – generally gale-force winds – a ship-of-the-line could outrun a frigate. Or a frigate could get unlucky, trapped between shore and a ship-of-the-line.) Only 45 times in 21 years did British and French frigates square off against each other in the single-ship combat beloved by authors – and readers – of nautical fiction.

There were reasons for this relative scarcity. A single-ship action required the presence of only two ships, but naval ships usually travelled in company with other naval ships. Fighting a single-ship action when sailing in a squadron or escorting a convoy required special circumstances, such as finding and pursuing a fleeing enemy until all other ships

Most readers today would associate a frigate duel with a scene like this one: valiant officers leading determined sailors over the bulwarks of their ship onto the deck of the enemy. (AC)

were out of sight. Even when a warship sailing independently encountered an enemy also sailing independently, naval combat was noisy. Despite the vast size of the seas, the places where ships are likely to be found are much narrower: headlands, straits, narrows and approaches to major seaports. The sound of gunfire frequently attracted other warships in the vicinity. Unless the battle was decided before other ships joined in, it was not a single-ship action.

Every British and French frigate captain dreamed of fighting – and winning – a frigate duel. There were monetary rewards for success. All navies paid prize money for captured ships, and the largest fraction went to the captains present when a prize was taken. In the Royal Navy, during the Great Age of Sail (1700–1825), the captains present split one-quarter of the prize money awarded. Money was not the main reward, however. A captured warship was usually worth less than a captured merchantman. A frigate captain sent commerce-raiding in waters filled with merchant ships carrying valuable cargos could quickly become a wealthy man.

Rather, the real reward of victory was glory. Winning a frigate duel – taking your ship into combat against an equally matched foe and emerging victorious – was the ultimate demonstration of a captain's professional superiority. It sealed a captain's reputation as a fighting man. Professional advancement also followed success. A victorious captain could receive promotion or have his officers promoted by an appreciative admiralty. A successful British frigate captain was often knighted, while a successful French captain

might have his name placed on a revolutionary roll of honour or, during Napoleon's Empire, inscribed in the Arc de Triomphe or even ennobled.

Victory also brought a captain fame and renown. Even defeated captains were accorded some measure of fame, especially when they fought long and hard against long odds. The public followed the results of naval combat in the same way that today's public follows the results of football matches. Successful frigate captains gained the same adulation as successful team captains do today.

The French Revolutionary and Napoleonic Wars represented an apogee for the sailing frigate and the frigate duel. It was the period at which the sailing frigate was at maturity, before being superseded by newer technology. It was also the last worldwide naval war fought without rapid communications, where decisions made by captains – even junior captains commanding frigates – could decide the fates of world powers. That autonomy was never greater than during a frigate duel – one reason that public fascination with them remains to this day.

Most naval actions were uneven fights. When MNF *Venus* attacked HMS *Ceylon*, the French ship was aided by the corvette *Victor*. After capturing *Ceylon*, the French lost their prize when a second Royal Navy frigate, HMS *Boadicea*, came upon the three badly damaged ships after the battle. (AC)

CHRONOLOGY

1789
5 May   French Revolution starts when the
               Estates-General meets for the first
               time since 1605.

1793
1 February   France declares war on
               Great Britain.
13 May   HMS *Iris* fights MNF *Citoyenne-
               Française* in the first frigate duel
               of the Franco-British wars fought
               between 1793 and 1815.
17 June   HMS *Nymphe* captures
               MNF *Cléopâtre*.
18 September   Britain and allies occupy Toulon.
1 December   Revolutionary France recaptures
               Toulon.

1794
1 June   Battle of the Glorious First of June.

A French naval sabre or cutlass of the late Napoleonic Empire. (Rama)

Spithead, as seen from Ryde on the Isle of Wight. Spithead was the main anchorage for the Royal Navy's Channel Fleet and the frigates assigned to it. (LOC)

1795
20 April — HMS *Indefatigable* captures MNF *Virginie*.

1796
21 December — French expedition sails from Brest in unsuccessful invasion of Ireland.

1798
1–2 August — Battle of the Nile.
14 December — MNF *Baïonnaise* captures HMS *Ambuscade*.

1799
28 February — HMS *Sybille* captures MNF *Forte*.

1801
6 July — First battle of Algeciras Bay.
12 July — Second battle of Algeciras Bay.

1802
25 March — Peace of Amiens signed, ending the French Revolutionary Wars.

1803
16 May — War between Britain and France resumes, starting the Napoleonic Wars.

1804
18 May — Napoleon declares himself Emperor of the French.

1805
21 October — Battle of Trafalgar.

1806
6 February — Battle of San Domingo.

1814
27 March — HMS *Hebrus* captures MNF *Étoile* in the final frigate duel of the Napoleonic Wars.
6 April — Napoleon abdicates, ending the war with Britain that started in 1803.

One month before the final frigate duel between HMS *Hebrus* and MNF *Étoile*, HMS *Eutoras* and MNF *Clorinde* fought a battle that lasted all night and left both frigates completely dismasted. When *Clorinde* attempted to escape under jury-rig, it was captured by two patrolling Royal Navy frigates. [AC]

DESIGN AND DEVELOPMENT

The term 'frigate' pre-dates the ship we now think of as the classic sailing frigate – a three-masted warship with its main battery on the upper gun deck and additional guns on the forecastle and quarterdeck. During the 17th century, 'frigate' described any warship built for speed and manoeuvrability. That usage survived through the 19th century in the class of merchantman known as the Blackwall Frigate.

The classic sailing frigate was a product of the 18th century, the result of efforts to improve cruising warships – ships intended for scouting, commerce protection and commerce raiding. Small cruisers were single-decked warships called sloops-of-war or corvettes. Depending on their size – which ran up to 22 guns – these ships were rigged with two or three masts. Although fast, large enough to capture a merchantman, and satisfactory as dispatch vessels in disputed waters, they were too weak to be satisfactory convoy escorts. Their small size limited their usefulness as scouts, as it restricted storage space and increased vulnerability to weather. A larger cruiser was required, one that could carry 24 to 44 guns.

As the 18th century began, two-deckers served as large cruisers. These had two full gun decks as well as upper works on which additional light guns could be carried. Small two-deckers carried between 28 and 44 guns. They could be thought of as miniature versions of ships-of-the-line. In the first part of that century 44-gun two-deckers often did stand in the line-of-battle, despite being thought of as too weak to be used for that purpose except at extreme need.

The problem with the cruiser two-decker was poor sailing characteristics, a product of geometry. The height of a man kept these ships too tall for their length, a problem

that worsened at the smaller end of the scale. The height of the gun deck had to remain constant to accommodate a sailor. The closer the lower gun deck was to the waterline, the more vulnerable they were to swamping. If the lower gun ports were closer than 4ft above the waterline, they could rarely be opened on the downwind side of the ship when seas were high. Those guns could only be used when the seas were calm – and when the wind was therefore too light for the high-sided small two-deckers to move quickly.

Eventually someone found a solution: eliminate the lower bank of guns. Eliminating the gun ports allowed the lower gun deck to be placed lower in the ship – as little as 1–2ft above the waterline. This allowed the upper gun deck to be moved down, too, and strengthened without the extra weight reducing the ship's stability. The battery that had been carried on the lower deck was moved to the upper deck, high enough so that the guns could be worked in virtually any seas.

The second deck of guns, the guns originally carried on the upper deck, was eliminated. These were lighter than the guns formerly carried on the lower deck, throwing a projectile that was between two-thirds and half the weight of the new upper-deck guns. Since the guns previously mounted on the lower deck could rarely be used, the swap effectively increased the broadside by at least 50 per cent.

Other benefits resulted from this change. This new design had fewer guns than a two-decker of comparable firepower. This reduced the number of crew required to load and fire the guns, making frigates more economical than small two-deckers.

A British 18-pdr frigate under sail. A frigate looked like a fast ship, and was always among the most beautiful naval warship types. (AC)

11

Reducing the berthing space that was required increased the volume that could be used for stores, yielding greater endurance. The crew could be accommodated in the now-empty lower gun deck, which was drier (and healthier) than the damp lower gun deck and submarine orlop of a two-decker. Finally, while the main battery was higher than that of a two-decker cruiser, the overall hull was lower, increasing speed, and reducing the ability of a crosswind to push the ship sideways. The result was a fast ship that had the same striking power as a two-decker cruiser, but was much more seaworthy. The new class was called a frigate, for it was fast and manoeuvrable.

Sailing frigates were full-rigged ships. They had three square-rigged masts known as, from front to back, the fore, main and mizzen. The square sails hung from spars attached perpendicular to the length of the ship. A boom called the bowsprit was also thrust out in front of the ship, angled roughly 30 degrees up. The masts were divided into sections. The lower mast was stepped (or anchored) in a block (the mast step), which for the fore mast and main mast was on the keel of the ship, and on the lower deck for the mizzen. The lowest square sail, the course, hung from a yard permanently fixed just below the lower mast's mast-top. Courses were only used on the fore and main masts. These were the largest sails on a frigate, and were cruising sails.

Above each of the lower masts was a topmast. These were attached to the front of the lower masts over a doubled area. At the bottom of this doubling was the mast top, a platform used to attach some of the shrouds – ropes guying the topmast. It was also used as a platform for marksmen during battle. The square topsail flew from the topmast. Topsails, although smaller than courses, were a frigate's main driving sails.

Above the topmast was the topgallant mast. This was attached to the front of the topmast over a doubled area. Instead of a top, at the bottom of this doubling was a grid of timbers known as the crosstrees. Again, shrouds used to hold the topgallant in place

BATTLE SAIL

Except for a few rare exceptions, frigates never fought battles with all sail set. Having every stitch of sail set strained the rigging, making the masts more vulnerable to damage from a single hit. Additionally, the lowest sails, the courses, were low enough to be set on fire by the muzzle flash of their own guns. Normally a warship went into battle under battle sail: topsails, outer jibs, and gaff sails set, with the courses brailed: pulled up in loose bunches under the spar. If winds were light, the topgallant sails could be set. If an extra burst of speed was needed, the courses could be shaken out, and then brailed back up again. This could be done from the deck, without taking the gun crews away from their guns for long.

A frigate, close-hauled, under battle sail. (AC)

Dating to the Seven Years' War, *Flore Américaine* was among the earliest generation of frigates. (Rama)

were attached at the ends of the crosstrees. The topgallant sail, smaller than the topsail, was attached to a spar on the topgallant mast. On most frigates, a fourth square sail was rigged above the topgallant. This was the royal sail. Sometimes the royal was mounted on its own royal mast, attached to the topgallant mast. More usually, it was attached to the upper part of the topgallant mast – set 'flying'.

The masts were held in place by stays that ran forward to the bowsprit and jib boom (for the fore mast) or to the mast ahead of it for the main and mizzen, and by backstays that ran to the sides of the ship behind each mast. Other lines, shrouds, ran to the top of the lower masts from the sides of the ship and provided additional support.

HMS *Minerva*, the Royal Navy's first 38-gun 18-pdr frigate, was a revolutionary concept that heralded the beginning of British domination in frigate design. (USNA)

Seaworthiness was a major advantage the frigate had over the small two-decker. It handled better in rough seas, as shown here, with the crew going aloft to shorten sail in stormy weather. (AC)

In addition to square sails, frigates carried a number of fore and aft sails. The most important of these were three to five triangular sails (called jibs or staysails) set from the fore-mast stays, and a large gaff sail aft of the mizzen mast. The gaff was attached to a gaff boom behind the top of the mizzen mast. By 1793 most frigates had a second boom at the bottom of the mizzen for better control of the gaff. The jibs and gaff were used to steer and turn the frigate. Trimming these sails increased or reduced the wind's thrust on them, allowing the ship to pivot about its centre of pressure – which, in a well-rigged frigate, would be near its main mast.

Like the 74-gun ship-of-the-line, the frigate was one of many French maritime developments of the 1730s and 1740s. *Médeé*, built for the *Marine nationale* and commissioned in 1741, is widely regarded as the first true sailing frigate. It carried 26 guns, with a main-deck battery of guns capable of firing an 8-pdr iron ball. The British captured *Médeé* in 1744, along with several other examples of this new class of French cruiser during the Wars of Austrian Succession (1740–48). Impressed with its sailing characteristics, the Royal Navy began building its own frigates before that war's end, copying the design of the captured French-built privateer *Tyger*. By the time the Seven Years' War (1756–63) started, the frigate had replaced the two-decker as a cruising warship for ships carrying 28 to 40 guns.

This first generation of frigates was small by the standards of the French Revolutionary and Napoleonic Wars. Most had a keel length of 100–110ft, and displaced 400–600 tons. They carried 28 guns: a main battery of 20–22 8-pdr (*Marine nationale*) or 9-pdr (Royal Navy) long guns, with 4-pdrs on the upper works. Typically a pair of 4-pdrs was mounted on the forecastle as chase guns, with the rest placed on the quarterdeck.

This class of frigate survived into the French Revolutionary Wars of 1793–1802, with some being built as late as the 1790s. Jack Aubrey's *Surprise* was one. (Although Aubrey is fictional, HMS *Surprise* was a real 28-gun frigate of that era.) So was MNF *Baïonnaise*, featured later in this book. Yet even at the start of these wars, the 28-gun frigate was viewed as too light to serve as a frigate, and by the start of the Napoleonic Wars in 1803, the *Marine nationale* rated its 28-gun ships as corvettes, rather than as frigates.

The Seven Years' War saw the introduction of the 32-gun frigate. Although only slightly longer than the 28-gun frigates (the Southampton class had a keel that was 102ft long), they were broader and heavier, displacing between 600 and 700 tons. They carried a main battery of 26 12-pdr guns with 6-pdrs on the upper works. The 12-pdr frigate had at least a 60 per cent superiority in firepower over the 9-pdr frigate. While a 12lb ball was only 33 per cent heavier than a 9lb ball, the additional kinetic energy it carried gave it half-again as much hitting power. Add in two extra main battery guns, and – all other things being equal – the 12-pdr frigate would always beat a frigate armed with 9-pdr guns.

The advantages possessed by the 12-pdr frigate quickly made it the standard heavy frigate of the Seven Years' War. It maintained this role, in a 32-gun and a larger 36-gun configuration, through the start of the American Revolutionary Wars of 1775–83 for both the *Marine nationale* and the Royal Navy. By the start of the French Revolutionary Wars it was considered a medium frigate. It was still the main type of frigate used during the French Revolutionary Wars, although most of these, including HMS *Nymphe* and *Ambuscade*, and MNF *Cléopâtre*, were built prior to 1793. HMS *Southampton*, launched in 1757, was still in commission in 1812.

The heavy-frigate role was being filled by frigates designed to carry an 18-pdr main battery. The idea for a frigate armed with a main battery of 18-pdr guns started in France, with proposals for these ships being put forward in 1775. This time, the British first put the idea into execution. Alarmed by reports that the French were considering construction of an 18-pdr frigate, in 1778 the British Admiralty ordered the construction of a new class of frigates – the 38-gun Minerva class.

It was revolutionary. Its design marked the beginning of British design ascendency over France. HMS *Minerva*'s keel was 117ft long, its gun deck 141ft in length. With a beam of 38ft, it displaced 940 tons. It needed the extra displacement because its scantlings (the hull's structural timbers) were heavier than those of previous frigates to permit it to carry 18-pdr long guns – 28 on its upper deck. It also mounted ten 6-pdr long guns on its upper works. Laid down in 1778 and launched in 1780, *Minerva* could outsail and outfight any frigate then on the ocean.

The French soon imitated the British, launching their first 18-pdr frigate in 1781. Slightly larger than British 38-gun frigates, and rated at 40 guns, these ships became the standard French heavy frigates in the 1780s. While both Britain and France built 12-pdr frigates after 1781 (including HMS *Pallas*, launched in 1804), the standard frigate during this period was the 18-pdr, quickly superseding the 12-pdr frigate. Even frigates intended to carry 32 or 36 guns were designed to carry an 18-pdr main battery. The captain of a 12-pdr frigate rated at 36 guns was at a disadvantage if the 32-gun frigate he fought mounted 18-pdrs, despite commanding the notionally 'larger' frigate.

Growth did not stop with the 18-pdr frigate. During the period between the American and French Revolutionary Wars, the *Marine nationale* began experimenting with frigates intended to carry a main battery of 24-pdr long guns. Two approaches were tried. Six small ships-of-the-line were converted to frigates, or razéed, by removing the quarterdeck and forecastle, and converting the upper gun deck into the new quarterdeck and forecastle. The lower-deck battery of 24-pdr guns was retained. At the same time the French designed and built a frigate intended to carry 24-pdr guns, *Pomone*. *Pomone* displaced 1,076 tons; its gun deck was 160ft long, and was to carry a main battery of 26 24-pdr guns. It was rated at 40 guns.

Britain initially ignored the 24-pdr frigate, but reports of these monster frigates stirred the Admiralty into action in the 1790s. In imitation of the French, it razéed three 64-gun ships-of-the-line – *Anson*, *Magnanime* and *Indefatigable* – into 44-gun frigates, each armed with a 24-pdr main battery. In addition, after capturing *Pomone* in 1794, the Admiralty used the lines for HMS *Endymion*, launched in 1797. To manage the larger guns, a 24-pdr frigate required a 30 per cent larger crew than an 18-pdr frigate. However, the Royal Navy kept capturing French 24-pdr frigates with their own 38-gun 18-pdr frigates, and decided that the larger frigate demonstrated the law of diminishing returns. They abandoned use of it by 1800, and *Endymion* was rearmed with an 18-pdr battery during its first commission of the Napoleonic Wars.

France kept building 24-pdr frigates through to 1812 – and kept losing them to smaller Royal Navy frigates. It was not until the War of 1812, with British losses to American 24-pdr frigates in frigate duels, that the Royal Navy reappraised its view of the 24-pdr frigate as a dead end. Between 1812 and 1815, Britain built or recommissioned over a dozen 24-pdr frigates.

Another major change occurred in the 1780s: the addition of a new type of armament to warships, the carronade. A short-barrelled gun mounted on a slide carriage rather than wheeled trucks, the carronade was developed by the Carron Company in 1775. They were much lighter than long guns: an 18-pdr long gun weighed 4,200–4,300lb, while an 18-pdr carronade weighed only 1,100lb. A carronade had a shorter range than a long gun, but since most battles were fought at ranges of 100yd or less, this hardly mattered. In 1779 the Royal Navy began adding carronades to all of its warships, initially 12- or 18-pdr carronades on the quarterdeck and forecastle in places where the decks

THE *OBUSIER DE VAISSEAU*

The initial French response to the carronade was the *obusier de vaisseau*. Bronze, rather than iron, the gun was adopted in 1787, and came in two sizes – one fired a 24lb ball and the other fired a 36lb ball. They were intended to fire an explosive shell, but the shells proved more dangerous to their users than their targets, and most captains used only solid shot with their guns. While sometimes called naval howitzers or sea mortars due to their short size, they were intended for direct fire, on a flat trajectory. The *obusier de vaisseau* was phased out after 1803, replaced with an iron 36-pdr gun similar to the British 42-pdr carronade. While they were in service, most French frigates carried four *obusiers de vaisseaux*, two on the forecastle and two on the quarterdeck.

A 36-pdr *obusier de vaisseau*. (Rama)

would not bear the weight of long guns. As a result, Royal Navy frigates carried eight to ten more guns than their rating would indicate. A 38-gun frigate mounted 38 long guns and ten carronades, or 48 guns in total.

Carronades gave the British a significant advantage during the American Revolutionary Wars, and the French soon added their own version of the carronade – the *obusier de vaisseau*. By the start of the French Revolutionary Wars both navies began replacing upper-deck long guns with carronades – typically larger carronades that each weighed as much as the long guns they replaced. At its battle with *Cléopâtre*, *Nymphe* carried 24-pdr carronades in place of all but two of its 6-pdr long guns.

L'Incorruptable was a 40-gun frigate of the *Marine nationale*, built in the 1790s. It saw service throughout the French Revolutionary and Napoleonic Wars, and was representative of the standard heavy frigate for the *Marine nationale* during this period. (AC)

The carronades weighed 1,456lb, compared to 1,800lb for a long 6-pdr. The trend continued throughout the period from 1793 to 1814, with more and larger carronades being added to the upper works. By 1803 the 32-pdr carronade was standard on British frigates, while the 36-pdr carronade was replacing the 8-pdr long gun on French frigates. The limiting factor on the growth of carronades was the weight of the ball. Although 68-pdr carronades were cast, 32–42lb was the heaviest load that one man could comfortably carry on the deck of a pitching ship.

This change in armament was facilitated by changes in the upper works of a frigate. Initially the forecastle and quarterdeck of the frigate were separate. To go from one to another involved going down a ladder to the upper deck, crossing the waist of the ship on the upper deck, and then climbing a ladder to go back up. By 1780 narrow gangways connected the forecastle and quarterdeck on most frigates. Gangways were light, intended only to carry a sailor's weight. Over time gangways widened and were strengthened. By 1814 they had widened enough to create a flush deck, called the spar deck, over the upper deck, and had been reinforced so that they would bear the weight of light guns, especially carronades. The 'double-banked' frigate, with a full deck of guns on the upper gun deck and a full deck of guns on the spar deck, was just appearing in 1814 but played no role in any frigate duel of the Napoleonic Wars.

Similarly, the sail plans of frigates grew in size between 1793 and 1814. The length of masts increased, allowing larger sails to be mounted on them. Royal masts became more common. During the period from 1793 to 1814 a fifth sail, the skysail, or even a sixth, the moonsail or hope-in-heaven, was occasionally rigged above the royal, although these sails generated little thrust and could only be used in the lightest winds.

The frigates used by the *Marine nationale* and the Royal Navy were similar. The Royal Navy fought numerous battles with frigates captured from the *Marine nationale* and subsequently added to the Royal Navy. The *Marine nationale* had fewer opportunities to return the favour, but did occasionally add British frigates to its numbers. Yet by 1793 there were differences between the frigates built by the two nations, outwardly invisible, but significant regardless.

THE FRENCH FRIGATE

French naval architects led the world in ship design during the first three-quarters of the 18th century. By 1780 they were losing their pre-eminent position. By the 1790s they had fallen into second place behind those of Britain, even though that reality would not be recognized – even by the British – until much later. This is not to say that the French were incapable of innovation. They pioneered the concept of the razéeing of a ship-of-the-line to convert it to a frigate in the 1780s, along with building the world's first 24-pdr frigates.

Rather, the failure was more one of execution. French naval architects were strong on theory, but less capable of translating their theoretical innovations into an optimal working design. An additional handicap was that the French were less willing to borrow shipbuilding concepts from other nations, especially after 1789. Great Britain (and later the United States) cheerfully adopted innovations from other countries, but French naval architects felt they had little to learn from others, due to their long period of engineering leadership. While France built frigates based on French innovations, Britain built frigates based on British *and* incorporating French innovations – a process that led to British superiority.

One example of this can be seen in the British *Endymion*. It was a copy of the captured French *Pomone*, but *Endymion* was built to Royal Navy standards, including heavier scantlings. The heavier *Endymion* could outsail *Pomone*. It was not a simple copy – it was an improvement on the design. Another example of French reluctance to adopt outside innovations can be seen in ship armament. Despite the obvious advantage that the British carronade offered, the *Marine nationale* was slow to adopt this innovation, and used it in smaller numbers than would be seen on its Royal Navy counterparts. Not until 1803 did France adopt an iron carronade, and only then did the French start deploying it in large numbers on their warships.

An additional feature retarding French ship development after 1789 was the French Revolution. The Revolution disproportionately affected the aristocrat-dominated Navy, with naval architectural innovation effectively frozen between 1790 and 1795. Even when resumed, it was directed towards efforts supporting Army goals (such as designing craft for the invasion fleet) rather than improving frigate design.

Even before the Revolution, differences between French and British frigates resulted from differences in available materials and in the different missions conceived by the two navies. France had more difficulty in finding naval timber than Britain, especially after 1780. Additionally, since France traditionally used its frigates for commerce raiding and scouting, rather than blockade duty, speed was viewed as paramount.

With its larger population, and because French iron-makers continued using charcoal well after British foundries had converted to coal, France experienced critical shortages in domestic timber, and had to import wood from elsewhere – as far away as Dalmatia and Russia. Its naval yards at Brest could only be reached by sea, and its yards at Toulon and Rochefort received most of their timber by sea. During wartime, blockade reduced the delivery of timber to a trickle.

A French 12-pdr long gun. Frigates mounting 12-pdr long guns as their main battery would be a staple of the frigate era, although by the end of the Napoleonic Wars, a 12-pdr frigate would have been considered a light frigate. (Rama)

MNF *CLÉOPÂTRE*

Length of gun deck: 145ft 7¾ in
Length of keel: 120ft 8⅞ in
Breadth: 37ft 8½ in
Depth of hold: 11ft 11¾ in
Displacement: 970 tons
Armament at battle: 28 12-pdr long guns, eight 6-pdr long
guns and four 36-pdr *obusiers de vaisseaux*. Total weight
of broadside: 264lb
Crew at battle: 320
Launched: Saint-Malo, 19 August 1781

Designed by the noted French naval architect Jacques-Noël
Sané, *Cléopâtre* carried a main battery of 12-pdr long guns.
Rated at 32 guns by the *Marine nationale*, it carried 36 long
guns in service, with four *obusiers de vaisseaux* added

in 1789. Launched in 1781, it served in Indian waters
during the American Revolutionary Wars, participating
in the capture of Cuddalore in 1782. Part of the Brest fleet
during the French Revolutionary Wars, it was part of French
naval forces in the English Channel in 1793. It was taken
after a brief duel with HMS *Nymphe* on 19 June 1793,
the first frigate captured in that conflict.

The Royal Navy had a *Cleopatra* so it entered the
Royal Navy as HMS *Oiseau*. It served as a frigate in
the Royal Navy from September 1793 through to 1801.
During that period it participated in the capture of ten
enemy ships. In 1806 *Oiseau* was converted to a prison
hulk, serving at Portsmouth. Laid up in ordinary in 1815,
Oiseau was sold in September 1816 and broken up.

One result of this was that in order to conserve wood, French naval architects used lighter scantlings and spaced the frames further apart on their frigates than was typical of other navies. This also made the hull lighter – which improved speed. It also made the hull weaker, allowing it to 'work' more when heavily loaded. This flexing of the timber weakened it further over time, reducing service life.

French designers compensated for this by making their ships longer so that the guns could be spaced further apart, reducing the load on the hull. Whereas the keel of a 32-gun British or Spanish frigate might be 100ft long and the keel of a 32-gun Dutch frigate 108ft long, a comparable French frigate would be 115ft. The higher length-to-breadth ratio created a slightly faster hull.

But it also made a ship more subject to 'hogging'. A ship floated because it displaced a volume of water equal to its weight. Its greatest volume was amidships and therefore the buoyancy force was greatest amidships, pushing the middle up more than the ends. The ends had greater weight than the midsection due to chase guns being placed at the bow and stern, pushing the ends down more than the middle. Over time this

HMS *Pomone*, launched in 1805, was a 38-gun 18-pdr Leda-class frigate. More Leda-class frigates were built for the Royal Navy than any other frigate design. (AC)

combination bent the keel into an arc, resembling a hunched hog. It also weakened the ship, leaving it more vulnerable to weather.

The *Marine nationale* compensated for this weakness by arming frigates intended for long cruises with lighter guns. An 18-pdr frigate sent to the Caribbean or the Indian Ocean would often be equipped with 12-pdr guns to ease the strain of the gun's weight. It also carried fewer stores, reducing loading problems, but also reducing endurance.

THE BRITISH FRIGATE

British shipwrights were designing and building the finest frigates in the world by 1800, on a par with, or maybe a little better than, the frigates built by American builders – USS *Constitution* and other Joshua Humphreys designs notwithstanding. This achievement was not realized at that time, but Britain had leapfrogged ahead of France in 1778, when it designed what would be the first 18-pdr frigate to be built, HMS *Minerva*. The design – for a 38-gun frigate armed with a main battery of 18-pdr long guns, and a keel 115–120ft long – proved the standard for heavy frigates for the next 35 years.

A characteristic of British frigate designs was that the ships were excellent sea boats and structurally sturdy. They were capable of remaining at sea for long periods of time even given rough weather, and were less likely to fall apart in a storm than their French counterparts. This was achieved by building hulls with a greater cross-sectional area than those of their French counterparts. The larger or fuller volume yielded allowed a British frigate to carry more stores, and made the ship more seaworthy in rough seas. Britain also used thicker timbers in the frames and spaced them more closely than other Continental powers (only the timber-rich United States used heavier scantlings than Britain).

Britain could afford to use heavier scantlings because it had greater access to shipbuilding timber than France. It had greater domestic resources because it had developed wood-conservation policies earlier than France and implemented them more effectively, even sowing plantations of oaks from the 1660s onward, which were mature enough to harvest for frigate construction by the late 1790s. Even as these ran out in the first decade of the 19th century, Britain, with its command of the seas, still had access to virgin shipbuilding timber such as teak and mahogany throughout the world. The British even had overseas shipyards capable of building frigates, especially in India.

There was a price to be paid for this. In theory, a full, heavy hull should move more slowly than the finer, lighter lines favoured by the French. All other things being equal, British frigates should have been slower than French frigates. Yet time after time, these theoretically slower British designs ran down their French rivals. The answer lay in a combination of superior masting and better seamanship.

A frigate's speed is not entirely a function of hull design. It also depended on a ship's sail configuration. The optimal location for the masts, and the optimal length of masts and spars, differed from ship to ship – even between frigates of the same class. Finding these locations and lengths was a matter of experience in sailing the ship.

The configuration of sails that yielded the best speed also changed as a function of wind speed and sea conditions. Too much sail could slow a ship as much as too little sail.

While a good hull could produce a good turn of speed, even without the optimal configuration of mast and sail, an indifferent hull design could match that speed given the proper mix of sails. British crews and captains, due to greater sea experience than their French counterparts, were more likely to know what yielded that result. Moreover, getting the best mix of masts and spars in a frigate was also a function of the masting timber available to the frigate. As with shipbuilding timber, the British had access to superior resources for masts and spars than did the French, especially by 1790, when the pine forests of Canada had fully replaced those lost with New England after the American Revolutionary Wars.

Yet while seamanship and masts allowed British frigates built to older designs to remain competitive, by 1795 British hull design had surpassed that of France. Even when British shipwrights used the lines from French prizes as the basis for their designs, they altered them. The result was a hybrid that merged French superiority in hydrodynamic theory with the British full-hull and heavier construction that was superior to earlier designs by both nations.

Additionally, British warships were more heavily gunned. A French frigate taken as a prize typically would enter the Royal Navy rated with more guns than those used by the *Marine nationale*. The Royal Navy typically added a pair of guns to the main battery, and often more on the upper works. Both *Nymphe* and *Cléopâtre* rated as 32-gun frigates when they were ships of the *Marine nationale*, but became 36-gun frigates when they entered the Royal Navy. The British were also more aggressive about adding carronades to the upper works. A British frigate almost always carried a heavier broadside than a comparable French frigate.

HMS NYMPHE

Length of gun deck: 141ft 5½ in
Length of keel: 120ft 4½ in
Breadth: 38ft 3¼ in
Depth of hold: 11ft 9in
Displacement: 937 $^{72}/_{94}$ tons
Armament at battle: 26 12-pdr long guns, two 6-pdr long
guns and ten 24-pdr carronades.
Total weight of broadside: 282lb
Crew at battle: 240
Launched: Brest, 18 August 1777

Designed and built by Pierre-Augustin Lamothe, *Nymphe*
was a 12-pdr French medium frigate, rated at 32 guns by
the *Marine nationale*. As part of the *Marine nationale* it was
at the First Battle of Ushant on 27 July 1778. *Nymphe* was
captured by HMS *Flora* in a single-ship action off Ushant
on 10 August 1780. Commissioned by the Royal Navy as

HMS *Nymphe* in 1781, rated at 36 guns, *Nymphe* served
as a repeating frigate at the battles of the Chesapeake
(5 September 1781) and the Saintes (9–12 April 1782).

Recommissioned in January 1793, as war with France
threatened, *Nymphe* was given to Edward Pellew, who
served as its captain until March 1794, capturing
Cléopâtre in a single-ship action on 19 June 1793.

After Pellew's departure, *Nymphe* remained in
commission under a series of captains through the Peace
of Amiens until wrecked in 1810. Extremely active, *Nymphe*
participated in the Channel Islands action on 23 April 1794
when three French frigates were captured, and participated
in the capture of the French frigate MNF *Résistance* and
corvette *Constance* on 9 March 1797. During the Peace
it remained in commission on anti-smuggling duty.
On 18 December 1810 *Nymphe* ran aground off Leith,
Scotland, and was wrecked.

THE STRATEGIC SITUATION

In early 1789 King Louis XVI of France called the Estates-General, France's counterpart to Britain's Parliament, into session for the first time since 1605. France was bankrupt, and additional taxes could only be raised through the Estates-General. At the time, France's *Marine nationale* was the world's second most powerful navy. A few years earlier it had fought the most powerful, that of Great Britain, to a standstill.

Instead of resolving Louis XVI's financial woes, the opening meeting of the Estates-General on 5 May 1789 started a train of events that overthrew the French monarchy and triggered the invasion of France by European land powers. On 21 January 1793, Citoyen Louis Capet, the former Louis XVI, was executed. Ten days later Republican France declared war on Great Britain, triggering a series of wars that would last almost continuously until June 1815.

By 1793, the *Marine nationale* was probably no longer the world's second navy, arguably surpassed by Russia and Spain. The ships were still there. It had 82 ships-of-the-line and 79 frigates divided between its three major naval stations at Brest, Rochefort and Toulon. A good half of them were ready or fitting for sea, and another quarter were in good condition. But the dockyards were in turmoil. Shipboard discipline had disintegrated amid revolutionary concepts of equality. A large fraction of the *Marine nationale*'s officer corps, almost all of whom were aristocrats, had fled France. The ones still at their posts, sympathetic to the Revolution, were generally the younger, less experienced officers.

The Royal Navy with which they were at war had 153 ships-of-the-line, 42 two-deckers (an intermediate class between ships-of-the-line and frigates) and

The execution of King Louis XVI led to an exchange of declarations of war between Revolutionary France and Great Britain. War would rage between the two nations for nearly two decades. (AC)

99 frigates. It also possessed the world's most professional officer corps to run its navy. In total, 251 captains, 167 commanders and over 1,350 lieutenants were available to command these ships. Most were veterans of the American Revolutionary Wars. Although most of Britain's ships were laid up when war was declared, with only 26 ships-of-the-line and 42 frigates in commission, that quickly changed. A year later 85 ships-of-the-line and 88 frigates were in commission – more than the *Marine nationale* possessed in total.

Considerably more, since 1793 was a disastrous year for the *Marine nationale*. The port of Toulon, home to one-quarter of the French fleet, had risen in support of the monarchy. While the city was retaken, an effort assisted by a then-unknown artillery officer, Napoleon Bonaparte, much of Toulon's fleet was destroyed and the port's facilities damaged. Between those losses, combat casualties and the hazards of the sea, the *Marine nationale* had lost 15 ships-of-the-line and 18 frigates by New Year's Day 1794.

The greatest loss was in the decline of the quality of its crews, however. The uprising in Toulon triggered a general purge called the Reign of Terror. Anyone suspected of Royalist sympathies was executed or imprisoned, including the aristocratic naval officers who remained after the defection of Toulon. They were replaced by merchant captains, familiar with ships but ignorant of combat, or warrant officers – capable within their specialities, but unfamiliar with the task of planning a battle.

Anything hinting of elitism was abolished. This included the *Corps de Cannoniers-Matelots* (literally, 'corps of artillerymen-sailors'), which provided the *Marine nationale* with its gunners. These specialists were replaced by soldiers, knowledgeable about artillery on solid land, but unfamiliar with the intricacies of effectively aiming artillery on a moving platform. The government reversed the decision a year later, but the damage was done. The naval-gunnery specialists were gone, absorbed into the French Army and replaced by new men who had to learn their trade anew. French naval gunnery never returned to the standards it achieved during the American Revolutionary Wars.

By the start of 1795, the French had dug themselves into a naval hole so deep they never emerged from it. Seamanship was largely a product of experience. Theoretical knowledge, which was possessed by *Marine nationale* personnel, produced competent performance. Even after the losses of 1793–94, the *Marine nationale* could likely have matched the navies of Spain, the Netherlands or any Baltic power. They were fighting the Royal Navy, however.

The early years of the French Revolutionary Wars scoured away the Royal Navy's inefficient and ineffective officers. The Royal Navy kept its ships at sea, especially its frigates. It had to. Loss of control of Britain's sea lanes would lead to defeat. Sea duty led to Darwinian selection. Experienced improved the quality of indifferent officers. Those lacking physical stamina retired or died. The incompetent removed themselves from the Royal Navy. They made errors that led to their removal despite the influence they wielded. If the Admiralty did not act, the implacable sea eliminated them.

Success bred more success. Britain always had more naval officers than seagoing slots for them to fill. Officers who achieved a reputation for aggressiveness and

The Royalist uprising at Toulon deprived the *Marine nationale* of its major Mediterranean naval base until its recapture following a three-month siege. The Republican assault that retook the port was aided by brilliant use of artillery by the young Napoleon Bonaparte. (AC)

The Arsenal at Brest. Brest was the *Marine nationale*'s largest naval base. Vulnerable because most of its supplies had to be brought in by sea, it was the focus of Royal Navy blockade during the wars. (AC)

competence were more likely to be employed than those without such reputations. This was especially true of the junior captains commanding cruisers, frigates and sloops-of-war. More time at sea meant more experience with their ship and in combat, which led to greater ability. A virtuous cycle developed.

France could have gone through the same process, especially during the period from 1793 to 1797. Britain was not imposing a close blockade on France during those years, and French fleets and frigates could – and did – sail at will. Inevitably, when they did, they encountered Royal Navy ships before they had acquired the experience that their foes had. But even when *Marine nationale* crews gained that experience it mattered little. France tended to send its ships on defined missions of limited length, such as the invasion fleets dispatched to Ireland in 1797 or Egypt in 1798, rather than keep them in commission over long periods, like Britain did. Even if a French frigate did achieve a level of efficiency comparable to one of its British counterparts, the crew would be broken up when its mission ended.

France never stopped trying. Between 1793 and 1798 it deployed cruiser squadrons to contest control of the English Channel and the Bay of Biscay. It sent the Brest fleet to North America to escort a grain convoy home, fought the British in the Mediterranean with a reconstituted Toulon fleet, and launched invasion fleets to Ireland in 1797 and Egypt in 1798. Along the way it acquired allies, conquering the Netherlands in 1795 and gaining Spain as a co-belligerent in 1797. The addition of the Dutch and Spanish fleets to the list of Britain's opponents at sea stretched the Royal Navy to its limits but never broke it. Instead, it defeated a Spanish fleet at Cape St Vincent and destroyed the Dutch Navy at Camperdown in 1797.

By 1798 France was returning to a strategy of *guerre de course*, the ineffectual strategy of commerce raiding adopted in the dying years of Louis XIV's reign. Britain began transforming its distant blockade to a close one, to pen the *Marine nationale* in port. The *Marine nationale* had shaken off the worst effects of the Revolution by then. It could have matched the Royal Navy of 1793, but not a Royal Navy hardened by five years of war.

By 1799 France had transformed from a revolutionary republic to a dictatorship run by Napoleon on the strength of his military victories. While Napoleon had restructured the *Marine nationale*, he thought of it as an auxiliary of the French Army. Although the *Marine nationale* had a few small successes between 1799 and 1801 (the capture of Elba and the First Battle of Algeciras) it never attempted a planned invasion of England. By the time the Peace of Amiens was signed in 1802, the Royal Navy ruled the seas.

The Peace of Amiens proved a breathing space for both Britain and France. War resumed in 1803. Napoleon used the peace to restore and reorganize the *Marine nationale*, building new ships and dispatching cruiser squadrons to the Caribbean and East Indies. Invasion of England was again threatened. In 1805, with the assistance of the Spanish fleet, Napoleon attempted to challenge the Royal Navy for maritime supremacy in a campaign that ended with the battle of Trafalgar. Napoleon marched the army intended for England into Central Europe and to glory at Austerlitz.

After one more attempt to put a fleet to sea in 1806, only for it to be captured by the British at the battle of San Domingo on 6 February that year, Napoleon attempted to defeat Britain through a trade war. Economic war thrusts by France and counterthrusts by Britain failed to cripple either power. Between 1805 and 1810

HMS *Amethyst* captures MNF *Niémen* on 6 April 1809. It was an action typical of the frigate duels of the Napoleonic era, involving a British frigate with a more experienced crew and a heavier broadside than its French opponent. (AC)

Britain achieved maritime dominance, capturing or neutralizing all enemy naval bases outside of Europe.

Trade warfare triggered two new conflicts in 1812. The War of 1812 erupted when the United States declared war on Great Britain over economic sanctions, and Napoleon invaded Russia that same year to enforce Continental trade restrictions against Britain. Britain got the better deal. America's naval efforts had minor effects, but Russia repelled the French invasion and put together a coalition including Sweden, Prussia and Austria that joined Britain and Spain (which had switched sides in 1807), conquered France in 1814 and forced Napoleon's abdication.

While the *Marine nationale* sent frigates out raiding between 1811 and 1814, the Royal Navy soon ran them down. Two decades of naval warfare between Britain and France effectively ended with Napoleon's first abdication in 1814.

TECHNICAL
SPECIFICATIONS

A frigate's ability to fight depended upon its ability to absorb punishment and keep on fighting, its ability to deal out damage, and its ability to manoeuvre and move. The first was a function of the ship's hull and its construction. The second was a function of its guns. The final category was a reflection of the ship's masts, spars and sails, the ability with which they could be used and how the frigate was trimmed. The ship with superior capabilities in these three areas generally won.

A frigate under construction in England. (AC)

THE HULL

The ability of a ship to absorb punishment was the function of its hull size and its construction. France had the advantage when it came to sheer size, building frigates that were larger than those of the British. The table overleaf compares the size of British-built and French-built frigates of different ratings.

Rating	Ship	Length of keel	Length of gun deck	Breadth	Depth of hold	Tonnage
28-gun	HMS *Fox*	99ft 6in	120ft 6in	33ft 6in	11ft 6in	594
	MNF *Baïonnaise*	103ft 4in	124ft 8in	32ft 8in	9ft 11in	598
32-gun	HMS *Ambuscade*	104ft	126ft 3in	35ft	12ft 3in	684
	MNF *Insurgente*	123ft 6in	149ft	37ft 5in	11ft 9in	850
36-gun	HMS *Caroline*	119ft	142ft 6in	38ft 3in	13ft 5in	924
	MNF *Cléopâtre*	120ft 9in	145ft 8in	37ft 8in	11ft 11in	970
38-gun	HMS *Minerva*	117ft	141ft	38ft 10in	13ft 9in	940
40-gun	MNF *Virginie*	126ft 3in	151ft 4in	39ft 10in	12ft 8in	1,066
44-gun	HMS *Indefatigable**	131ft 10in	160ft 10in	44ft 5in	13ft 3in	1,150
	MNF *Sybille*	127ft 1in	152ft 3in	40ft 6in	12ft 4in	1,090

*HMS *Indefatigable* was razéed from a ship-of-the-line. Tonnage is calculated for its service as a frigate.

The table above compares frigates built in the 1780s and 1790s to each other, and attempts to use ships built within five years of each other. French-built craft tended to be larger and shallower. Only *Indefatigable*, a razéed ship-of-the-line, was larger than a French-built frigate of a comparable gun rating. However, the Royal Navy built no 44-gun frigates until 1813, only acquiring these ships through capture or conversion from ships-of-the-line. Those post-1813 ships were larger than the French 44-gun frigates of the 1790s.

Plugging shot holes after a battle. The ability to absorb damage was a characteristic of a successful frigate design. (AC)

While the French had the advantage in size, British-built ships had the advantage in construction. An 18-pdr long gun could penetrate 42in of white oak at 30yd, while a 12-pdr long gun could penetrate 30in of white oak at that distance. Other woods, including red oak and elm, had less resistance than white oak. It took ten per cent more red oak to provide the same stopping power as white oak.

The keel of a British frigate was between 13¼in and 15½in wide with corresponding frames that at the floor (or bottom) of the hull were 85 per cent the width of the keel, tapering to 60 per cent of the keel's width at the top of the hull. A 28-gun frigate would have frames varying from 8in to 11in, while a 38-gun frigate's frames would range between 11in and 13in in thickness.

THE GREAT GUNS

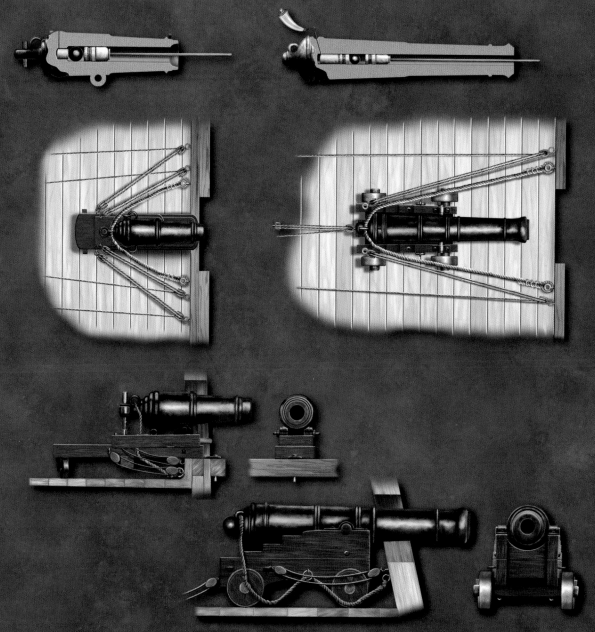

Frigates carried two major kinds of great gun during this period: long guns [right] and carronades [left, not to scale]. While some frigates still carried main batteries of 12-pdr and 9-pdr long guns, the 18-pdr long gun was the gun of choice for frigate built after 1790. The barrel of an 18-pdr gun weighed 4,200–4,300lb, and could throw an 18lb iron ball 1,200yd. The bore was a constant diameter throughout.

The first carronades mounted on frigates were 12- and 18-pdr carronades. The size quickly grew. From the mid-1790s, most British frigates carried 32-pdr carronades. These guns weighed 2,000lb (roughly the weight of a 9-pdr long gun), but had a bigger punch than the upper-deck long guns they replaced. Carronades had a chamber smaller than the bore for the powder charge. The French carried 36-pdr brass *obusiers de vaisseaux* or iron carronades on their frigates.

A long gun, run out for action. This gun is fitted with a flintlock, although a slow match would be available in case of a misfire. (AC)

British shipwrights placed a frigate's frames at 28in to 30in intervals, leaving a space of 18–20in between the edges of each frame. The exterior of the frames would be covered by a sheathing of planking 3–6in thick. British-built frigates were typically built using white oak for the structure, although red oak or various pines were used if ships were needed quickly, and ships built elsewhere (especially in India) were constructed with teak or mahogany.

French shipwrights had trouble finding adequate white oak during peacetime, much less when the British were blockading the French coast. France had fewer stands of native oak than Britain. As a result, French construction often used imported wood, inferior to that available in Britain, and French shipwrights placed a greater reliance on red oak.

Combined with the fact that this timber hunger also led French shipyards to build frigates with lighter frames than their British counterparts, and to space the frames further apart, it would be fair to say that a French-built frigate had 80–90 per cent of the structural integrity of a corresponding British-built frigate. It was one of the reasons that France had been slow to adopt the 18-pdr frigate. An 18-pdr long gun weighed one-third more than a 12-pdr long gun, requiring correspondingly heavier scantlings.

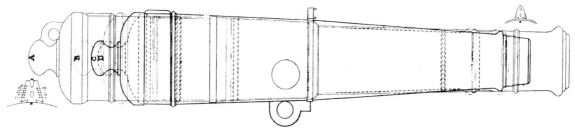

COMPARISON OF THE ORDINARY LONG AND SHORT 24-PRS. WITH THE CONGREVE AND THE SHORT BLOMEFIELD 24-PRS.

(*See* p. 16.)

A. Long 24-pr., length, 9 ft. 6 in.
B. Short 24-pr.
C. Congreve 24-pr.
D. Blomefield short 24-pr.

THE GUNS

The main battery of a frigate generally consisted of a battery of smoothbore, muzzle-loading long guns. On its upper works, the quarterdeck and forecastle, it carried a mixture of long guns and carronades. By the start of the French Revolutionary Wars, four different types of long guns were carried by frigates on their main deck: 9-pdrs (8-pdrs on *Marine nationale* frigates), 12-pdrs, 18-pdrs and 24-pdrs.

The size of guns, for both long guns and carronades, referred to the weight of the shot that the gun fired. The size of a gun mounted was a function of the weight of the barrel of the gun. At the start of the French Revolutionary Wars both Britain and France used pounds for weights and feet for length. It is anachronistic to refer to French artillery in metric terms prior to 1799, when France introduced the metric system. Traditional French weights were still commonly used throughout the Napoleonic era. However, the British (or Imperial) and French systems were different. French measurements were generally larger than the British. One French royal *livre* (or pound) equalled 1.08 of the British pound avoirdupois used by the Royal Navy. Similarly, the old French royal *pied* (foot) equalled 1.066 British feet. The table that follows shows the weight of French shot in French and British measurement systems.

Weight of French shot		
French gun	Weight of shot (livre)	Weight of shot (avoirdupois)
8-pdr	8	8.63
12-pdr	12	12.95
18-pdr	18	19.42
24-pdr	24	25.90
36-pdr	36	38.85

This is one reason captured ships were rearmed with guns cast for the victorious nation. A French 12-pdr ball was too large to fit in the bore of British 12-pdr cannon. A British 12-pdr ball was too small to be fired effectively from French 12-pdr cannon, for too much of the propellant gases would escape between the gap, or windage, between the ball and the bore of the gun.

Four different designs for a 24-pdr long gun. The largest was the standard design in 1793. The shortest – the Blomfield – was light enough to substitute for a standard 18-pdr. These designs were the outgrowth of fresh developments in artillery design that followed the development of the carronade. (AC)

RECEIVING AND DELIVERING FIRE

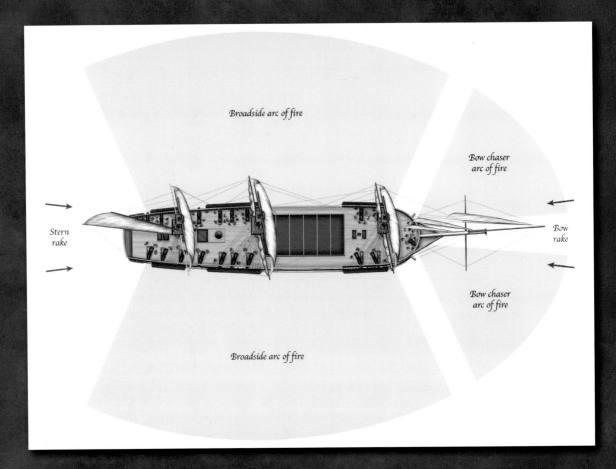

Broadside arc of fire

Bow chaser
arc of fire

Stern
rake

Bow
rake

Bow chaser
arc of fire

Broadside arc of fire

Part of the art of fighting a frigate battle was placing your ship where your guns could hit your opponent to maximum effect, without your opponent being able to fire at you. Since most of the guns on a frigate ran along the side of the ship, and could pivot only about 22 to 30 degrees, that meant a frigate's arc of fire for these guns ran in a 45- to 60-degree arc off its beam. To fire this 'broadside' of guns you had to manoeuvre so that your foe was roughly perpendicular to your direction of travel.

Your chances of victory improved if you could manoeuvre so that you could fire at your foe while remaining out of the enemy's arc of fire. The most devastating results occurred when you lined up your ship so that it could fire a raking broadside the length of the enemy ship – either through its bow, where only its two bow chasers could respond, or through its stern, with its vulnerable glass galleries. Often, one or two broadsides fired from a raking position could decide a battle.

SAILING A FRIGATE

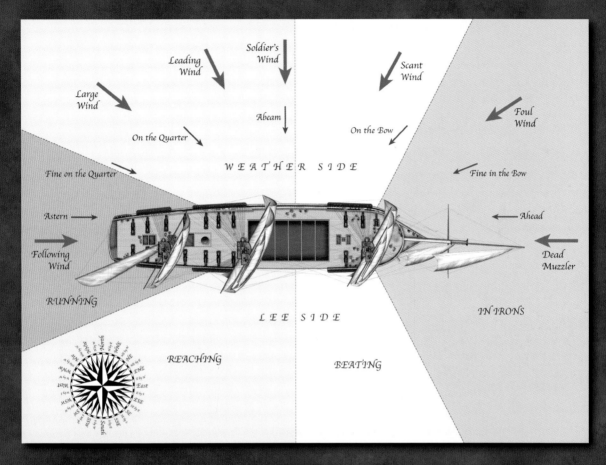

The relative wind direction, as well as its strength, determined how fast a frigate could sail. A wind from astern was a following wind, and the ship would be 'running before the wind'. A wind on the beam from behind was a large or a leading wind (depending upon the angle) and a ship favoured with these winds, right on up to a wind coming from directly abeam (a soldier's wind) was said to be 'reaching'.

A wind ahead of the beam was a scant wind. Twisting the spars on which the sails were set allowed a frigate to catch some of this wind, and move the ship forward slowly, 'beating' into the wind. With the wind still more forward – somewhere between 30 and 45 degrees from the bow – it became foul. The sails would not fill, and the ship went in 'irons'. A wind directly ahead was a dead muzzler.

A ship's fastest speed came when it was reaching. When it was running, the after sails would blanket the sails ahead, reducing their thrust. The best point of speed varied from ship to ship, depending upon the positions of its masts and how the ship was loaded.

Dockyard sheer legs being used to install lower masts on a frigate during its fitting out. (AC)

Any long guns carried on the upper works fired a ball that weighed roughly half of that employed by the main battery. British 9-pdr frigates mounted 4- or 6-pdrs, while French 8-pdr frigates mounted 4-pdrs; 12-pdr frigates carried 6-pdrs on their upper works, while 18-pdr frigates carried 6- or 9-pdr long guns. The relatively few British 24-pdr frigates carried 9- or 12-pdr guns on their upper works, while the *Marine nationale*'s 24-pdr frigates mounted 8-pdr long guns.

The upper works also included carronades – or for the *Marine nationale* during the period from 1793 to 1804, brass *obusiers de vaisseaux*. At the start of the French Revolutionary Wars, light and medium frigates in the Royal Navy were generally carrying 24-pdr carronades, with the heavy 18-pdr frigates mounting either 24- or 32-pdr carronades. French medium and heavy frigates, and some light frigates, carried 36-pdr *obusiers*, with some light frigates mounting 24-pdr *obusiers*.

The carronade represented a new look at artillery design. It was possibly the world's first scientifically designed gun, and perhaps the first artillery piece designed as part of a weapons system. A new method of boring cannon had been developed by the Carron Company in Scotland, and that process applied to developing the carronade.

Carronades were bored to tighter tolerances than standard long guns, with the result that carronades had less windage. They also used a chamber for the powder charge that was smaller than the bore of the gun. The result was that the ball flew with greater accuracy and using a smaller charge than it would if fired from a long gun of the same bore rating. The carronade's barrel was shorter than that of a long gun, and tapered – it was narrower at the muzzle than at the breech – without the muzzle flare characteristic of the long gun. The result was a weapon that was much lighter than a long gun and more accurate over the course of its trajectory.

Carronades had a shorter range, but since most sea fights at that time were fought at ranges of 100yd or less, this was unimportant. Although a carronade was inferior to a long gun firing the same-sized ball, it generally replaced smaller cannon or was added in a place that could not bear the weight of a long gun. Swapping a 4-pdr long gun for a 24-pdr carronade improved a ship's firepower.

Ironically, the carronade's accuracy gave it a perhaps undeserved reputation for inaccuracy. Little live-fire practice at targets was done during this period. Most was done with long guns. Most gunners simply aimed along the top of the barrel to sight their shot, depending upon experience (usually gained on long guns) for the required elevation. Sighting along the top of a carronade's tapered barrel meant that its shot would go high – high enough to fly over a target ship's deck at ranges in excess of 200yd. After 1800, captains began adding sights to carronades to correct this, but by that date the gun's reputation for inaccuracy was well established. In any event, new artillery such as Blomfield guns and Columbaids, guns developed as a result of the lessons learned in designing the carronade, offered superior performance to the carronade.

Carronades and *obusiers* were initially added to the battery of long guns carried on the upper works, on parts of the quarterdeck and forecastle too lightly built to place long guns. At the start of the French Revolutionary Wars, the *Marine nationale* still adhered to this policy. Light frigates carried two *obusiers*; medium and most heavy frigates carried four. The heaviest French frigates, the 18-pdr 40-gun frigates and especially the 24-pdr 40- and 44-gun frigates, would carry six to eight *obusiers*.

By 1793 the Royal Navy had already begun replacing some of its upper-deck gun decks with carronades, and also replacing the authorized carronades with larger ones. While a 36-gun 12-pdr Royal Navy frigate was authorized to carry six 18-pdr carronades, most carried ten to 14 24-pdrs, cramming in an extra pair above the six carronades authorized, and exchanging as many as eight of the authorized 6-pdr long guns for carronades.

As the war continued, the French followed suit. By 1794 *Pomone* had exchanged all but two of its upper-works 8-pdrs for 36-pdr *obusiers*. The British kept adding carronades and using carronades of larger sizes as the war continued. By the start of the Napoleonic Wars in 1803, most Royal Navy frigates had replaced almost all of the guns on the upper works for 32-pdr carronades, retaining two or four long guns as chase guns. The *Marine nationale* was replacing its brass *obusiers* with iron 36-pdr carronades. Lighter guns were carried only when the ship's age or structural weakness prevented the use of larger carronades.

THE RIGGING

Frigates moved under sail. How fast they could move and how quickly they could manoeuvre depended upon the strength of their masts and spars. Mast timbers required flexibility. Softwoods, especially resinous pine and fir, make the best masts. The strongest masts came from pole masts, carved from the trunk of a single tree.

The size of available timber – both in terms of diameter and length of the tree – limited the size of a pole mast. A large frigate's main mast might be 100ft long and 30in in diameter. If pines of that length and diameter were unavailable, 'made masts' were substituted. A made mast used a central pole, or spindle, surrounded by wedges cut from smaller trees bound together with iron hoops. While not as strong as a pole mast, using a made mast was better than using a shorter and thinner pole mast.

As with other marine timbers, the advantage in finding mast timbers went to Britain. In addition to domestic resources, Britain drew upon the pine forests of Canada and imported Baltic Sea timbers taken from Scandinavian and Russian forests, while France got its masts and spars either from the Baltic or the Pyrenees. These timbers had to travel by sea – even masts coming from domestic sources. This left the *Marine nationale* pinched for masts. Those available were frequently smaller and of lower quality than those available to the Royal Navy. Even when France built hulls that could outsail British frigates, the *Marine nationale* could not outfit its frigates with masts capable of exploiting that advantage.

THE COMBATANTS

Without men to operate them, ships are useless. This was never truer than for a sailing frigate. No ship sails itself. It requires a crew to operate the ship and work her guns, proficient officers to command her, and determined soldiers (in the form of marines and, for the French, gunners) to fight her. More often than not, victory in a frigate duel was due less to the quality of the frigate than to the quality of the frigate's crew.

THE MEN

A frigate carried between 90 and 190 sailors. These men set and trimmed the sails, steered the ship, operated the guns and maintained the ship in a seagoing state. The hands did the tasks, while petty officers – themselves skilled sailors – supervised the hands.

Sailors started young – often as young as ten. Sailors who could handle (knew the ropes that controlled the sails), reef (work the sails, and change their size through reefing) and steer (operate the helm) were considered skilled seamen. In the Royal Navy they would be rated an able seaman. In the *Marine nationale* such a man was called a *loup de mer* (sea wolf).

Topmen, shown working aloft furling a sail, were the aristocracy of a frigate's sailors and were always in short supply. (AC)

41

During wartime the Royal Navy used impressment to man its ships. Here a British officer is impressing a sailor, who claims American nationality, off a merchant vessel. (AC)

Most prized were topmen, who worked aloft. A frigate needed at least two dozen topmen in each watch, and no frigate ever had enough. The job required strength, agility and intelligence. A single mislaid line could result in a failed manoeuvre and cost a battle. It was a young man's game; most topmen were in their teens, and few were older than 30.

Older sailors worked on deck, handing the lines, controlling the sails, manning the helm or doing other skilled tasks that could be done on deck. This included supervising the inexperienced sailors on simple tasks. While much aboard a frigate required skill and experience, there was also much that simply required strength. Newcomers – landsmen or *matelote d'eau douce* (freshwater sailors) – or the dull-witted could pull on the gun tackles, haul on rigging lines from the deck or handle the capstan that raised and lowered the anchor, if supervised by experienced sailors.

Advancement was possible. The most experienced topman on a mast directed operations as captain of the top, while the sailor in charge of a gun would be a gun captain. Sailors assisting a ship's various specialists – the carpenter, cooper, sailmaker, boatswain, gunner and master – could become mates. In these positions they would learn the responsibilities of these jobs and in time advance into those positions by obtaining a warrant – moving into warrant rank. Additionally, master's mates could and did earn commissions as lieutenants. Petty rank was assigned by the ship's captain. A sailor could be rated or de-rated at will. Other petty officers aboard a frigate included cook, master-at-arms (responsible for maintaining discipline), the surgeon's mates (medical orderlies) and clerks.

The Royal Navy and the *Marine nationale* recruited their sailors differently. Recruitment in Britain was decentralized (especially when the war started in 1793), while France had a more centralized and bureaucratic method of manning ships. The Royal Navy drew crews from individual volunteers and impressment. During peacetime, it depended almost exclusively on individuals volunteering to serve

By 1800, manpower shortages led the Royal Navy to curtail shore leave. Instead, when in harbour, the men were put at easy discipline and allowed visits from 'wives'. The result is shown in this period print. (AC)

aboard a warship. A man joined a ship rather than the Royal Navy, signing on for a cruise – typically three years – and becoming a civilian when the ship went out of commission.

Even during wartime, volunteers were important, but the vast increase in the fleet meant too few volunteers were available. The Royal Navy fell back on impressment, a practice that started when the king would impress merchant ships and their crew into service. By 1793, only crews were still being impressed. When manpower was needed, a shore-based Impressment Service scoured British ports for seamen, seizing sailors unlucky enough to be caught. These were sent to receiving ships, and held for ships needing men. Individual ship captains also impressed sailors – either by sending a party ashore or by boarding a merchant ship and taking members of its crew. Only British mariners could be impressed – landsmen were of limited value. Some mariners, such as fishermen, were exempt from impressment. Citizens of foreign countries could volunteer if they wished, but could not be impressed. Of course, when an English-speaking sailor claimed United States citizenship, lines blurred.

SIR EDWARD PELLEW

One of the foremost Royal Navy frigate commanders of the wars with France between 1793 and 1815, Edward Pellew, 1st Viscount Exemouth, led a life that reads as if taken from a nautical adventure novel. He was born on 19 April 1757 in Dover, where his father commanded a Dover packet. His family was Cornish and returned to Cornwall after the death of Edward's father in 1764.

Pellew entered the Royal Navy as a midshipman in 1770 aboard the frigate *Juno*, served aboard *Alarm* in the Mediterranean, and then on the frigate *Blonde*, which took General John Burgoyne to America in 1776. Detached to serve on Lake Champlain in 1776, Pellew fought at the battle of Valcour Island on 11 October 1776 aboard the schooner *Carleton*. He took command when his superiors were injured and was rewarded with permanent command of *Carleton* following the battle.

In 1777, as part of a Royal Navy contingent, Pellew accompanied Burgoyne's expedition to New York. He fought at Saratoga and became a prisoner when the British army surrendered. Released on parole, Pellew was promoted to lieutenant on 9 January 1778 after returning to England, and given a post aboard a guardship, *Princess Amelia*, until exchanged. In 1779 he served as lieutenant

Admiral Sir Edward Pellew,
1st Viscount Exmouth, GCB. (AC)

aboard the frigate *Licorne* and in 1780 was appointed to *Apollo*.

On 15 June that year *Apollo* fought a large French privateer, *Stanislaus*. *Apollo*'s captain was killed early in the battle, and Pellew took command, dismasted *Stanislaus* and drove the privateer ashore. He was promoted to commander, and rewarded with command of *Hazard*. In 1782 he took command of *Pelican*. On 28 April, while commanding *Pelican*, he fought three French privateers off Brittany and drove them ashore. He was promoted to post-captain and appointed to *Artois*, a 40-gun 18-pdr frigate. After less than a month in command of *Artois* he captured a large frigate-built French privateer.

Pellew spent the peace between the American and French Revolutionary Wars on half-pay except for a

As the French war dragged on, fewer British mariners volunteered (naval service appeared to be becoming a life sentence rather than a three-year affair) and impressment yielded too few bodies. In 1795 Parliament passed the Quota Act, requiring counties to deliver a quota of men annually to the Royal Navy. Most were landsmen, but despite legend few were criminals. The Royal Navy refused criminals except for smugglers (who were often mariners).

France had an organized system of naval conscription: the *Inscription Marine*. All Frenchmen who served in a maritime profession for at least a year were to register on the *role des gens de mer* (roll of mariners) at age 18, and annually thereafter. They were assigned to a department (typically the one closest to where they lived) and were subject to call-up for service in the *Marine nationale*. When they were called up depended upon family status. The levy in each department was divided into four classes: unmarried men, widowers without children, married men, and heads of households. Unmarried men were called up first, with heads of households conscripted only after all other groups had been exhausted. Evading call-up marked the sailor as a deserter.

The French system worked so long as naval ships did not remain in commission for long periods of time. The *Marine nationale* tended to commission ships for individual missions, rather than keep them in service continuously. However, there were rarely

OPPOSITE A *loup de mer* of the *Marine nationale* at the topmast mast top. [AC]

three-year term as captain of the frigate *Winchelsea*. After war with France started in 1793, Pellew was appointed commander of *Nymphe*, a 32-gun frigate. He quickly got the ship ready for sea, and on 18 June sailed from Falmouth, in search of two French frigates reported in the English Channel. The next day he found MNF *Cléopâtre*, and captured it in a short fight. He was knighted for the action.

In January 1794 he was transferred to *Arethusa*, a 38-gun frigate armed with 18-pdrs. While serving as *Arethusa*'s captain he fought in three actions between British and French frigate squadrons in the English Channel. Over the course of these the French lost four frigates, including MNF *Pomone*, a 44-gun frigate, which was captured by *Arethusa*.

In January 1795, Pellew was rewarded with command of the 44-gun *Indefatigable*. *Indefatigable* had been razéed from a 64-gun ship-of-the-line, and carried a main battery of 24-pdr guns. While commanding *Indefatigable* Pellew captured the 40-gun French frigate MNF *Virginie* in a single-ship action on 20 April 1795. On 21 December 1796 Pellew and *Indefatigable* spotted the French fleet sortieing from Brest to invade Ireland. Attacking, Pellew scattered them. Three weeks later, on 13 January 1797, *Indefatigable* caught the 74-gun *Droits de l'Homme* returning to Brest. With the assistance of *Amazon* (36 guns), Pellew fought

the ship-of-the-line in a full gale, driving it ashore – the only successful defeat of a ship-of-the-line by frigates during that period.

In March 1799 he was given command of *Impétueux*, a 74-gun ship-of-the-line, which was in bad discipline. On 30 May, while *Impétueux* was in Bantry Bay with the fleet blockading Brest, a general fleet mutiny was attempted, starting on *Impétueux*. Pellew crushed the mutiny, preventing a general uprising. He commanded *Impétueux* until the peace in 1802.

Promoted to rear admiral in 1804, Pellew was sent as naval commander-in-chief in the East Indies. There until 1809, Pellew directed Royal Navy efforts to protect British merchant shipping and defeat French naval and privateering in the eastern seas. He returned from the Indies as a vice-admiral. In 1810 he commanded the North Sea Fleet and in 1811 he was appointed commander-in-chief in the Mediterranean. On 14 May 1814 he was created Baron Exemouth as a reward for his services, and on 4 June 1814 promoted to admiral.

In 1816 Pellew saw combat for a final time, leading a British naval expedition to Algiers. On 27 August 1816 he bombarded Algiers, defeating that Barbary state, and forcing it to abandon piracy. From 1817 to 1821 Pellew was commander-in-chief at Plymouth, and then retired from active naval service. He died on 23 January 1833.

enough mariners to man an entire fleet, leading to large numbers of landsmen aboard French warships, and to French frigates having crews with less experience working together as a team than British frigates did.

THE OFFICERS

A frigate was run by four to six commissioned officers, and eight warrant officers. These men directed the ship's crew. They were assisted by midshipmen – junior warrant officers who were officers in training. A frigate might carry as many as six midshipmen.

The most senior officer aboard a frigate was the captain. In the Royal Navy, the job typically fell to a junior captain. (The Royal Navy had three commissioned ranks at that time: lieutenant, master-and-commander and captain. All captains held the same rank with seniority deciding superiority.) In the *Marine nationale*, a frigate was usually commanded by a *capitaine de frégate* (frigate captain), although the more senior *capitaine de vaisseau* (ship-of-the-line captain) or more junior *lieutenant de vaisseau* (senior lieutenant) might be assigned command.

A captain ran the frigate. He was accountable only to his admiral, typically aboard another ship, or directly to his nation's admiralty, in London or Paris. Aboard ship, the captain's word was law. He could rate or dis-rate crew members, arrest officers and order men punished. His commands were to be obeyed instantly. He did not stand watches, but was on call at all times. While his frigate was in commission he was expected to live aboard it even in harbour, except when granted permission to take leave by his superiors.

He directed operations from the quarterdeck, which gave the best view of the ship he commanded. It was also the most exposed position in the ship during battle. Casualties among those on the quarterdeck – especially officers – ran high.

He was assisted in running the ship by three to five lieutenants, holding commissions as officers issued by the nation for which they fought. The Royal Navy kept things simple with only one grade of lieutenant. The *Marine nationale* had two ranks for lieutenant: *lieutenant de vaisseau* (senior lieutenant – literally 'ship-of-the-line lieutenant') and *enseigne de vaisseau* (junior lieutenant). Within their ranks British and French lieutenants were ranked by seniority – the length of time that they had held their commission.

The most senior lieutenant aboard a ship served as first lieutenant – the executive officer, second in command to the captain. Like the captain he did not stand assigned watches, although a good first lieutenant would take a watch if the frigate was short of qualified watch-keeping officers. In combat, his normal station was the quarterdeck, by the captain, where he could take command if the captain became incapacitated, or lead special activities such as a boarding party if so directed.

The remaining lieutenants stood watches, each running the ship during a four-hour period in lieu of the captain or first lieutenant during everyday operation. A frigate's crew was typically divided into two divisions, which manned the watches alternately. One of the watch-keeping lieutenants was assigned charge of each division. In combat, these lieutenants commanded the gun deck. The two most senior would command the starboard and port main batteries, and if any other lieutenants were carried they would command the guns on the upper works.

Subordinate to the commissioned officers were warrant officers. These men were senior technical specialists who were in charge of different aspects of running the ship. Instead of commissions they held warrants. In the Royal Navy, these warrants were issued by different boards. In the *Marine nationale*, appointments came from the admiralty in Paris.

While the titles and some responsibilities differed, regardless of nationality a frigate had a similar set of warrants: a master (responsible for navigation), a boatswain (in charge of the masts, rigging and deck operations), a carpenter (in charge of the hull), a cooper (responsible for the barrels which stored provisions and water), a gunner (responsible for the ship's guns and ammunition), a purser (responsible for provisions) and a surgeon (responsible for the crew's health). Sometimes a frigate carried a schoolmaster or, on a Royal Navy frigate, a chaplain. (The *Marine nationale* was officially atheistic during the Revolutionary period.)

Superior to everyone else, except the warrant and commissioned officers, were the officers in training; they were known as midshipmen in the Royal Navy or *aspirants* in the *Marine nationale*. They held warrants rather than commissions. Their job was to learn how to be an officer. Their tasks, assigned by the officers, included standing watch with the lieutenant of the watch, handling the signal flags, serving as messengers and commanding the ship's boats. In combat they commanded the men in one of the three fighting tops, or a section of guns.

After acquiring enough sea time (six years in the Royal Navy) and passing an examination, a midshipman would receive a lieutenant's commission. A midshipman might be made acting lieutenant when a vacancy occurred, but this rank was not confirmed until the examination was passed. While most midshipmen were in their teens – even as young as 12 – a slow-witted or unlucky man might remain a midshipman into his twenties or thirties.

The Royal Navy drew its officers primarily from the gentry or the British middle class. The Royal Navy was the closest thing to a meritocracy Georgian England had, with significant upward mobility possible. The primary reason for this was the hazards associated with the sea. While influence played a role in promotion, a captain had to sleep – and he slept better with a competent if low-born officer commanding the deck rather than an aristocratic ninny. Noble-born officers were relatively rare until after 1805, when the Navy became 'fashionable'.

Prior to the Revolution virtually all *Marine nationale* officers were aristocrats. Noble birth was a requirement for a commission prior to the 1770s, although occasional waivers were issued. Many of these aristocrats left France prior to 1793, and many of the rest were purged during the Reign of Terror or left French service after Toulon declared for the king. Revolutionary France initially tried to make up the shortfall with the few remaining pre-war officers (occasionally offering a choice between resuming command and execution), by promoting warrant officers or commissioning merchant captains and mates. The *Marine nationale* never recovered from these purges, even when a more regular system of identifying and recruiting potential officers emerged after Napoleon took over. Developing competence as a naval officer required experience at sea. During the war years, the Royal Navy prevented French officers from acquiring the necessary experience, and the months of peace in 1802–03 proved to be too short.

THE MARINES

Both Royal Navy and *Marine nationale* frigates carried contingents of soldiers aboard. Both sides used marines – as these sea soldiers were called – to maintain discipline aboard ship and provide musketeers and boarders. The marines provided sentries that guarded officers' cabins, and during battle they guarded hatchways to keep unauthorized men from avoiding their duty by hiding below. Marine infantrymen were stationed on the fighting tops and along the bulwarks of the forecastle and quarterdeck during battle, to serve as snipers. When not required for these duties, they could be used for hauling on deck – either rigging line or gun tackles. Marines could not be used to handle rigging aloft however, unless they volunteered.

CHARLES-ALEXANDRE LÉON DURAND, COMTE DE LINOIS

One of the most successful French naval officers during the period 1793–1814, Charles-Alexandre Léon Durand, Comte de Linois was born in Brest, France on 27 January 1761. Known today primarily for his activities as an admiral in the Mediterranean and East Indies, he commanded frigates in several actions and as an admiral fought one campaign primarily with frigates.

Linois entered the *Marine nationale* as an *aspirant de marine* (midshipman) in 1776. During the American Revolutionary Wars he served aboard ships in the English Channel, Spanish waters, the West Indies and Île de France (now Mauritius).

Promoted to lieutenant in 1789, he was posted to the East Indies, where he remained until 1794. One of the few pre-revolutionary officers in the *Marine nationale* following the Revolution, his East Indies posting kept him out of France during the Reign of Terror.

After returning to France he was given command of MNF *Atalante*, a 32-gun 12-pdr frigate. While cruising off Cork, in company with the corvette *Levrette*, Linois spotted a British merchant convoy, and closed seeking merchant prizes. The convoy was escorted by two British ships-of-the-line, one of which, HMS *Swiftsure*, set off in pursuit of *Atalante*.

After a two-day pursuit, *Swiftsure* caught *Atalante* on 7 May 1794. Although Linois fought, *Swiftsure* soon forced the frigate's surrender.

Linois was soon exchanged, his reputation undiminished by his defeat due to the unequal odds and his stiff defence. He gained command of *Formidable*, a 74-gun ship-of-the-line. As part of the Brest fleet in May 1795, *Formidable* fought at the battle of Groix on 23 May, and was one of three ships-of-the-line captured by the British. Linois was badly injured, losing an eye, and again taken prisoner.

Again quickly exchanged, Linois was given command of MNF *Unité*, a 36-gun 12-pdr frigate. On 13 April 1796, while carrying the household of the governor of Rochefort to Brest, *Unité* was spotted by Pellew's squadron off Ushant, which pursued. HMS *Révolutionnaire* outstripped the rest of Pellew's squadron, and caught *Unité*. Outgunned in weight of metal nearly 2:1, *Unité* quickly surrendered.

Exchanged again, Linois was promoted to *chef de division* (roughly equivalent to the Royal Navy commodore). He commanded a squadron during the *Expedition d'Irlande*, the French attempt to invade Ireland, but the squadron was scattered by Pellew when it sailed from Brest in December 1796. Linois reconstituted his squadron, which successfully

Officers lived lives considerably more luxurious than common seamen. Here they are shown dining aboard ship in the captain's cabin (note the cannon, covered with cloth). The price for this life was greater risk in combat. (AC)

reached the landing spot off Bantry Bay, but the landing was cancelled after the rest of the fleet failed to appear.

Promoted to *contre-admiral* (rear admiral) in 1799, Linois became second-in-command of the French Mediterranean fleet under Ganteaume. Linois participated in the capture of Elba, and then was sent with an independent squadron of ships to Cadiz. That squadron won the First Battle of Algeciras Bay on 6 July 1801, capturing HMS *Hannibal*, a 74-gun ship-of-the-line. The French squadron was joined by a Spanish squadron of ships-of-the-line, fighting the Second Battle of Algeciras Bay, a night-time action, on 12 July 1801. Its disastrous outcome (two Spanish three-deckers fired on each other until both exploded) did not weaken the reputation Linois had gained through the victorious first battle.

Immediately prior to the collapse of the Peace of Amiens, Linois was sent to command French forces in the Indian Ocean. With his flagship, the 74-gun *Marengo*, and a number of frigates and corvettes, he harried British shipping for the next three years. While generally successful against superior British naval resources, Linois's eastern service is best remembered for a failure, when Linois's squadron caught the China Fleet of Indiamen off Pulo Aura in 1804. The lightly armed Indiamen should have been easy prey, but the convoy's commander had disguised the largest Indiamen as ships-of-the-line and formed a line-of-battle,

challenging Linois to battle. Convinced by the bluff, Linois retired.

Following the British capture of the Cape of Good Hope in 1806, Linois decided to return to France with what was left of his squadron – *Marengo* and one frigate, *Belle Poule.* En route, the ships encountered a British squadron and were captured. Napoleon

Charles-Alexandre Léon Durand, Comte de Linois. (Rama-PD)

refused to exchange Linois, and Linois remained in captivity until the war's end in 1814. Napoleon did create Linois as Comte de Linois in 1810, however, and Linois's name was inscribed on the Arc de Triomphe.

After the Restoration, Louis XVIII made Linois governor of Guadeloupe, but Linois supported Napoleon during the Hundred Days, and was forced to resign after Waterloo. Acquitted in a subsequent court-martial in 1816, Linois was forced to retire. Although appointed as an honorary vice-admiral in 1825, he was never employed again by the *Marine nationale*. He died on 2 December 1848 at Versailles, where he had been living.

Marines in the *Marine nationale* also had responsibility for supervising artillery operations aboard ship. This included overseeing the sailors working the guns, and aiming and firing the great guns, tasks done in the Royal Navy by a senior sailor known as a gun captain. This reflected a difference in philosophy in the two navies. France viewed the use of ordnance – artillery as well as muskets – as primarily an army responsibility, and placed soldiers aboard ship to supervise their operation. Britain viewed the artillery aboard a warship as an integral part of the ship, and assigned responsibility for their use to the crew of the ship.

A Royal Navy frigate carried a contingent of 38 to 45 marines. These soldiers were drawn from one of three regiment-sized divisions in what from 1793 through to 1802 were His Majesty's Marine Forces. They did not become the Royal Marines until 1802. Each contingent consisted of a marine lieutenant who commanded the frigate's marines, a marine sergeant, one or two corporals and 34 to 40 privates.

Because the marines aboard *Marine nationale* ships combined the function of infantry and artillery, the marine contingent of French frigates was always larger than those of British frigates – from 60 to as many as 120 men. Part of this was due to French marines serving at the guns. However another reason was that France always had more soldiers available than sailors. They would add soldiers to the crew on the grounds that additional musketry might help win a battle. *Marine nationale* frigates were also used to move soldiers between garrisons. Adding an extra 50–100 soldiers to a *Marine nationale* frigate sailing for the Caribbean or Mauritius was viewed as an economical way of reinforcing colonial garrisons or returning time-expired soldiers.

The names, organization and functions of *Marine nationale* marine units frequently changed between 1793 and 1814. At the beginning of the period their infantry was drawn from the fusilier regiments of the *Corps de Cannoniers-Matelots*. These regiments were abolished in 1794 and absorbed into the army, which then provided the marines to French warships. Then in 1795 the marine artillery was restored, creating seven demi-brigades of marine artillery from which warships could draw contingents to serve as experienced gunners and shipboard infantry. Over the next ten years, these forces would be reorganized four more times. A final reorganization in 1813 transferred control of the corps from the *Marine nationale* to the French Army.

One of the duties of a frigate's marine contingent was to participate in boarding actions, including cutting-out operations such as the one shown here, where an enemy ship was attacked using the frigate's small boats. (AC)

COMBAT

Four frigate battles are featured in this book. These featured battles are in some ways unrepresentative of the kind of frigate duel typically fought between British and French frigates during the French Revolutionary and Napoleonic Wars: a duel between two 18-pdr frigates. Yet each of these battles illustrates a different and important aspect of single-ship combat. The first is a duel between two evenly matched opponents eager for combat for its own sake. The battle between HMS *Nymphe* and MNF *Cléopâtre* was probably the most evenly matched contest between a British and French frigate during the French Revolutionary and Napoleonic Wars – and one of the relatively few fought by mutual consent of the two captains.

The second battle, fought between HMS *Indefatigable* and MNF *Virginie*, was a classic chase. A pursuit that lasted over half a day was required to force the combat. The battle was atypical in that *Indefatigable* was armed with 24-pdrs and so was one of a handful of super-frigates in the Royal Navy of the day. Yet it was a typical frigate duel in other ways. The more powerful frigate won, which, as presented in the Statistics and Analysis chapter, was the typical outcome of a single-ship action. It was also influenced by the presence of other ships, also a common occurrence. *Virginie* ran not just from *Indefatigable*, but from two other British frigates accompanying *Indefatigable*.

The battle was fought exclusively between *Indefatigable* and *Virginie* – the accompanying frigates having been sailed under the horizon by the two combatants. Although *Virginie* had effectively been defeated by *Indefatigable* prior to the eventual reappearance of the other British frigates, *Virginie*'s surrender was motivated by this – a common outcome in British and French frigate duels.

The third action, that between HMS *Ambuscade* and MNF *Baïonnaise*, was decided by small arms and boarding. While many single-ship actions were settled when one frigate boarded the other, in most cases gunnery had disorganized and demoralized the crew of the defeated frigate before the first boarder set foot on it. In the fight between *Ambuscade* and *Baïonnaise*, *Ambuscade* had won the gunnery duel and *Baïonnaise* attempted boarding as a desperate attempt to avoid defeat. It was a virtually unique example of this technique succeeding and the only battle in which an inferior French warship captured a superior British opponent.

The fourth action, that fought between HMS *Sybille* and MNF *Forte*, is included for several reasons. Both ships were built in the 1790s, and represented the state of the art of frigates during the wars covered. The battle illustrated two of the main functions of frigates during these wars – commerce raiding and commerce protection. *Forte* was hunting British Indiamen, while *Sybille* was seeking to stop *Forte*. It also illustrated why the Royal Navy stuck with the 18-pdr frigate. *Forte* was armed with a main battery of French 24-pdr guns, yet *Sybille* apparently easily beat *Forte*. It took the War of 1812 and the United States Navy's 24-pdr frigates to reverse that judgement.

NYMPHE vs CLÉOPÂTRE

The war between France and Britain was not even five months old on 18 June 1793. Even so, the two frigates that fought that day, HMS *Nymphe* and MNF *Cléopâtre*, set a pattern for the frigate duel which real frigate captains attempted to repeat through the next quarter-century, and nautical-fiction authors would imitate for the next two centuries.

It was an action that was among the most balanced of the wars that followed. There was little difference between the two ships. Both had been launched from French shipyards, within five years of each other. They had identical main batteries – 26 12-pdr long guns. Both had scratch crews, called into service after the war began, yet each had had a few months to knock experience into their men. While *Nymphe* had the heavier broadside, *Cléopâtre* had a larger crew.

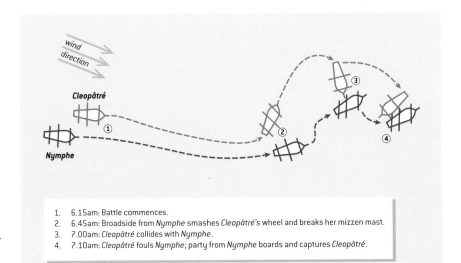

This map shows the battle between HMS *Nymphe* and MNF *Cléopâtre* on 18 June 1793. It traces the track of both ships and illustrates the major events during this frigate duel.

1. 6.15am: Battle commences.
2. 6.45am: Broadside from *Nymphe* smashes *Cleopâtré*'s wheel and breaks her mizzen mast.
3. 7.00am: *Cleopâtré* collides with *Nymphe*.
4. 7.10am: *Cleopâtré* fouls *Nymphe*; party from *Nymphe* boards and captures *Cleopâtré*.

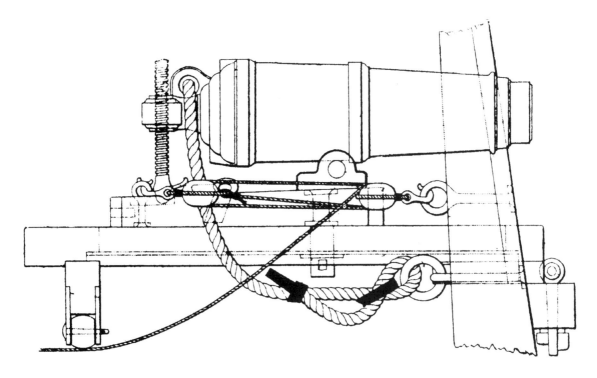

Even their captains had similar backgrounds. Edward Pellew of *Nymphe* commanded frigates in the American Revolution and in the peace that followed. Jean Mullon of *Cléopâtre* was newer to command, but still a professional naval officer. A *lieutenant de vaisseau* prior to the war, he had been rewarded for his loyalty to the Revolution with command of a frigate. It was the same type of jump Royal Navy lieutenants occasionally made when taking command of their first frigate.

HMS *Nymphe* had replaced most of its quarterdeck and forecastle 6-pdr long guns with 24-pdr carronades, like the one shown here. (AC)

NAVAL TIME

During the period of the French Revolutionary and Napoleonic Wars, standard time zones lay in the future. All time was local. The naval day began at noon – defined at the instant at which the sun reached the highest point in the sky. Unlike today, it always occurred midway between sunrise and sunset or – at the speed of a sailing ship – close enough to midway between sunrise and sunset as to not really make a practical difference. Daylight savings or meridian shifts did not yet exist. Sunrise and sunset at sea occur when the centre of the sun is six degrees below the horizon. For the man on lookout duty, dawn began when he could make out a grey goose at the distance of a nautical mile.

A naval sextant, used to determine local noon during the age of fighting sail. (AP-HMM)

These frigates had played cat-and-mouse since late May, chasing each other in the English Channel. *Cléopâtre* and a companion frigate, MNF *Sémillante*, had operated out of Cherbourg since May, with British frigates vainly pursuing. Pellew had sailed from Falmouth the previous day hoping to find one of them. Shortly after dawn, at 3.30am the next morning, Pellew spotted a sail 15 miles from Start Point.

Nymphe chased the sail, which proved to be *Cléopâtre*. Initially, the French frigate fled. Yet *Nymphe* proved faster, or perhaps Mullon preferred combat once he realized that *Nymphe* was alone, offering an even fight. At 5.00am, *Cléopâtre* hauled up. Furling up topgallants and hauling in the fore course, *Cléopâtre* awaited the approach of the British frigate.

A sea fight under battle sail is fought at the pace of a jogging man. *Nymphe*'s approach took an hour. Both ships cleared for action, striking unnecessary gear below, wetting down and sanding the decks, loading the guns, sending the crews to their combat stations. It is likely that both crews had breakfast, despite the early hour. Men fight better on a full stomach. Regardless, both crews were ready, even eager, for action.

Pellew took the lee gage, opting to place his ship downwind of *Cléopâtre*. It was an unusual choice for a British ship. Most British captains preferred the upwind weather gage, so that they could swoop down on their opponent. Perhaps Pellew wanted to cut

The climax of the battle between *Nymphe* and *Cléopâtre*, with *Cléopâtre* running foul of *Nymphe*. (AC)

N.BROWN,SC.

Cléopâtre off from retreat, placing *Nymphe* between *Cléopâtre* and France. Taking the lee gage did not affect *Nymphe*'s speed. The wind was blowing from the after quarter, and the two ships were near their fastest point of sailing. Nor did Mullon intend to flee. He wanted to fight, waiting as *Nymphe* approached.

At 6.00am, *Nymphe* was close enough for Pellew to watch Mullon address *Cléopâtre*'s crew. Mullon waved a red cap of liberty as he spoke. Pellew hailed *Cléopâtre*. Mullon responded, but Pellew did not hear what was said. Pellew shouted 'Hoa! Hoa!' and *Nymphe*'s crew gave three cheers. In response, Mullon shouted 'Vive l'Nation!' and *Cléopâtre*'s crew replied, shouting 'Vive l'Republique!' Mullon gave the cap of liberty to a sailor who climbed up the mast and nailed the cap to the mast head.

Fifteen minutes later, *Nymphe* drew alongside *Cléopâtre*. Pellew, who had been standing bareheaded, put his hat on his head, the signal to commence firing. Mullon, also bareheaded, did the same. A furious exchange of broadsides commenced, with the two ships barely 50yd apart. British gunnery soon told. At 6.30am Mullon turned *Cléopâtre* away from *Nymphe*, to increase the range. The turn exposed *Cléopâtre*'s starboard stern quarter to *Nymphe*'s fire, while taking *Nymphe* out of *Cléopâtre*'s line of fire. Undisturbed by French artillery, *Nymph* swept *Cléopâtre* with a devastating broadside, deciding the battle. One shot, probably a 24-pdr ball from a quarterdeck carronade, struck *Cléopâtre*'s mizzen mast, severing it 12ft above the deck. A second round shot struck the wheel, destroying it. A ball also struck Mullon, ripping open his back and hip.

Cléopâtre's mizzen mast tumbled down. The wind pushed the sails of the fore mast downwind. Without a countering torque from the wind pushing the mizzen sails, lost with the mast, *Cléopâtre*'s bow swung downwind, turning the ship towards *Nymphe*. Loss of the wheel kept the rudder, pivoting freely, from countering the swing.

The fate of the captured crew of the losing frigate in a frigate duel was captivity. They did not escape the sea even in captivity, however, as naval prisoners were usually kept aboard prison ships, as shown in this print. (AC)

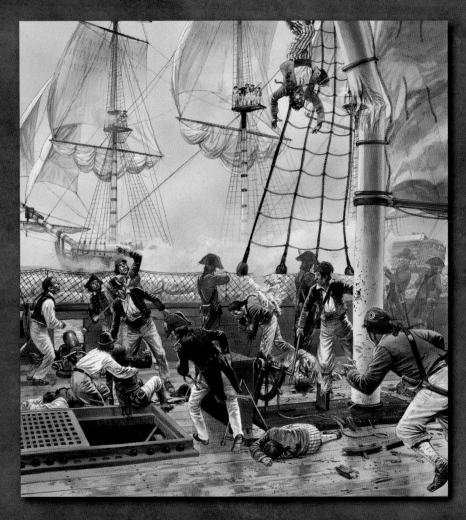

At 6.30am, a bare 30 minutes after the battle between *Nymphe* and *Cléopâtre* began, HMS *Nymphe* fired a broadside that decided the engagement. One shot struck *Cléopâtre*'s mizzen mast 12ft above the deck, severing it. A second shot struck the wheel, shattering it. The hits made steering *Cléopâtre* impossible, as both the rudder and steering sails were lost. As a result, the uncontrollable *Cléopâtre* abruptly turned, taking *Nymphe* out of its line of fire. Worse, a round shot struck *Cléopâtre*'s captain, Jean Mullon, fatally wounding him.

This plate shows the confusion on *Cléopâtre*'s quarterdeck in the wake of the broadside. The wheel is gone and the helm crew dead or wounded. The mizzen mast is collapsing, dooming those in the mast top or working its sails to a fall onto the deck or into the water – unless they are lucky enough and quick enough to move to the still-standing main mast or slide down the mizzen backstays to safety. Mullon is refusing to leave his post despite his injuries, and attempting to command the ship despite being too injured to stand. *Cléopâtre* continues sailing, rudderless and temporarily leaderless, but not in the direction its captain wants it to go.

Meanwhile, only 25yd away – close enough for a pistol shot to reach – stands *Nymphe*, firing yet another controlled broadside into the vulnerable *Cléopâtre*. Within ten minutes, *Cléopâtre* will foul *Nymphe*, allowing Pellew the opportunity to board and take the disorganized and now demoralized French frigate.

QUARTERDECK VIEW – HMS *NYMPHE*

On the quarterdeck of HMS *Nymphe* the battle at 6.45am looks considerably better than it does from the quarterdeck of the French *Cléopâtre*. After exchanging broadsides for 15 minutes, *Cléopâtre* suddenly fell away from *Nymphe*. While this increased the range between the two ships, it also allowed *Nymphe* to fire on *Cléopâtre*'s exposed quarter without *Cléopâtre* having *Nymphe* in its arc of fire. Unmolested by anything more than musketry from *Cléopâtre*'s marine contingent, Pellew pours round shot into his opponent for 15 minutes. Then, at 6.45am, a British broadside strikes *Cléopâtre* with decisive results.

Pellew, standing calmly on his quarterdeck, directing the action, can see part of the result of that broadside. *Cléopâtre*'s mizzen mast, severed by a shot, can be seen collapsing. Another shot has struck *Cléopâtre*'s wheel. The loss of the helm, combined with the loss of the steering sails on the mizzen mast, renders *Cléopâtre* uncontrollable. Pellew's foe is also leaderless as a result of the broadside, something that Pellew would not know directly but which he could infer from the disorganization that he observes on the French frigate.

In a few minutes, *Cléopâtre* will turn towards *Nymphe* and, driven by the wind, strike *Nymphe* amidships. In the meantime, Pellew continues to have his ship pour a rapid and disciplined cannonade into the hapless *Cléopâtre*. By the time the ships touch *Cléopâtre* will prove easy prey for a British boarding party.

Nor was there anyone fully in charge of *Cléopâtre* any more. Mullon remained on deck, attempting to rally his crew, but his wounds were mortal, too severe for clear thinking. Steered only by the wind at 7.00am, *Cléopâtre's* bow rammed *Nymphe*, *Cléopâtre's* bowsprit striking between *Nymphe's* fore mast and main mast. *Cléopâtre* twisted to starboard, until the two frigates lay broadside to broadside in opposite directions, *Cléopâtre's* bowsprit splintering as it struck *Nymphe's* main mast. As the ships lay head to stern, *Cléopâtre's* anchor hooked in *Nymphe's* main mast shrouds. Combined with the damage done to the main mast by *Cléopâtre's* bowsprit, this threatened to bring it down.

With the two ships locked together, Pellew ordered his crew to repel boarders. As his men left their guns and formed for hand-to-hand combat, Pellew noticed the disorder aboard *Cléopâtre*. Instead of defending *Nymphe*, he ordered the French frigate boarded. A small party of British boarded *Cléopâtre* through the main deck gun ports. Among their number was Israel Pellew, Edward's younger brother, serving aboard as volunteer.

Though badly outnumbered, this party fought their way up to and along *Cléopâtre's* gangways, to take the quarterdeck. At 7.10am, less than an hour after the firing commenced, British sailors hauled down the French ensign. *Cléopâtre's* demoralized crew fled below, and the battle was over.

Cléopâtre was the first French frigate captured by the Royal Navy. British reaction was unrestrained celebration. Pellew was knighted for the victory. His brother, Israel Pellew, was promoted to captain. *Nymphe's* first lieutenant was made a commander.

INDEFATIGABLE vs *VIRGINIE*

Few frigate duels were as even as the one fought between *Nymphe* and *Cléopâtre*. Generally there was some disparity in a frigate duel, and they usually ended with the victory of the larger ship. One example of this was the battle fought between HMS *Indefatigable* and MNF *Virginie* on 20 April 1796.

Indefatigable was a 44-gun razée frigate, one of three frigates the Royal Navy converted from 64-gun ships-of-the-line by cutting down the upper gun deck. It had a 24-pdr main battery, and a ship-of-the-line's scantlings. Commanded by Sir Edward Pellew, *Indefatigable* was then part of a five-ship squadron led by Pellew, patrolling the western approaches to the English Channel. A week earlier, the squadron had encountered *Unité*, a 12-pdr frigate commanded by the future Comte de Linois, off Ushant. After a pursuit, the 38-gun HMS *Révolutionnaire*, an 18-pdr frigate, captured *Unité* following a brief fight on 13 April.

By the 20th, Pellew's squadron was down to three ships: *Indefatigable* and the two 36-gun frigates, *Amazon* and *Concorde*. *Révolutionnaire* had taken its prize to Britain, and *Argo*, a 44-gun two-decker, had gone to Plymouth to reprovision. The three frigates had weathered The Lizard, a peninsula of Cornwall, when a strange sail was sighted. *Indefatigable* ran up the private signal, a combination of signal flags to be answered by a different combination by the challenged ship. A British warship, with its signal book, would know the challenge and response.

The strange sail was not a Royal Navy warship, however. It was MNF *Virginie*, a 40-gun 18-pdr frigate, cruising in the western approaches. While the equal of the 18-pdr *Amazon* and superior to the 12-pdr *Concorde*, *Virginie* was inferior to *Indefatigable*.

Regardless of the merits of the individual British ships, *Virginie*'s captain, Jacques Bergeret, recognized that his ship was no match for the combination of the three unidentified warships, which were almost certainly British. Ignoring the signal, he turned away from the British frigates, hoping they would assume he had not seen it. Instead, the British pursued. The French and British frigates all added sail, *Virginie* seeking the safety of Brest, and the British attempting to catch the fleeing French frigate.

A stern chase is a long chase – this one was more than usually long. At speeds that exceeded 11 knots, for 15 hours and 168 miles, the pursuit continued. *Amazon* and *Concorde* fell behind *Indefatigable* and *Virginie* until only the two larger frigates were in sight of each other, with *Indefatigable* slowly gaining. The wind shifted slightly, trapping *Virginie* against Ushant on the Breton coast of France.

At midnight, *Indefatigable* came within gunshot of *Virginie*. For the next hour and 45 minutes both ships raced along under full sail, exchanging broadsides at close quarters. A night-time action imposes some of the most difficult conditions in which to fight. Except when the guns are firing there is no illumination and when they do fire, muzzle flash destroys night vision. Everything – sail handling, loading and firing the guns, bringing up fresh cartridges from the magazine – must be done by touch, with results briefly seen as the guns blaze. As a result, despite the close range – the two ships were within 100yd of each other – accuracy was poor on both sides.

A frigate hove-to. The fore and mizzen sails are pushing the ship forward, while the main sails are backed. Without a main topmast a frigate loses the capability to do this effectively. (AC)

Yet damage did accumulate. *Virginie* lost its main topmast and its mizzen mast in the exchange of broadsides. *Indefatigable*'s mizzen topmast was shot away, as was its gaff, and the lines controlling its main topsail. The exchange of damage actually favoured the *Virginie*, however. It began to fall behind *Indefatigable*, slowed by the loss of sail, and *Indefatigable* could not back sails to remain abreast. Backing sail required the main topsail spar to be twisted so that the sail pushed against the mast, while the mizzen and fore sails continued to push the ship forward. Done right, the manoeuvre would slow the frigate without turning it. The loss of its main topsail and all of its mizzen sails prevented the right combination of sails from being used, and so *Indefatigable* shot ahead of *Virginie*.

Bergeret now had an opportunity frigate captains dream of – the chance to stern-rake his opponent and fire an entire broadside down the length of an enemy warship. A successful rake would disable *Indefatigable*, allowing *Virginie* to escape, with the possibility of capturing *Indefatigable* before the other British frigates could join the battle. As *Indefatigable* shot past, he turned *Virginie* so as to cross the stern of his opponent.

While most of the French shot had gone high, into *Indefatigable*'s rigging, much of *Indefatigable*'s fire had been aimed at *Virginie*'s hull. *Virginie* had taken several shots near the waterline, and was taking on water – by the end of the battle, the lowest 4ft of the hull was filled with water. It, too, had lost steering sails. Its turn across

CLEARING FOR ACTION

A warship was as much a home as it was an instrument of war. Officers lived on the upper gun deck in removable cabins beneath the quarterdeck. Warrant officers and senior petty officers lodged beneath the forecastle. Other equipment, necessary to the everyday operation of a ship, was also kept on the gun deck. When it went into action, it was necessary to remove these objects in a process called clearing for action.

Everything not needed for combat – partitions, furniture, carpeting, tools – would be sent to the hold. This removed

obstacles to working the guns and reduced the number of objects on the gun deck that could become projectiles if struck by a cannonball. Decks would be wetted down to damp out any sparks that might land, and would be sanded to improve footing. Sponge tubs would be filled with water, and the lashings that secured the guns removed so that guns could be run out. Muskets would be issued to marines and marksmen, and the racks holding the boarding weapons unlocked.

The gun deck of a frigate, shown as it would appear when cleared for action. (Rama-PD)

Indefatigable's stern was sluggish, the French ship slowed by its waterlogged hull, and its ability to manoeuvre hampered by the loss of the mizzen mast.

Pellew was aware of his peril. While he could not slow his ship, he could turn it. As *Virginie* turned, *Indefatigable* followed the turn, keeping its stern gallery out of *Virginie*'s field of fire. The two frigates drifted apart, like two exhausted boxers, out of gunshot of the other. But *Indefatigable* was downwind of *Virginie*. The French frigate could not run because *Indefatigable* was in the way, and neither frigate could sail into the wind due to the damage sustained aloft.

Both ships set to repairing their rigging. *Indefatigable* was winning that race, having set new lines that allowed it to use its topsail braces, when the *Concorde* appeared. It had been out of sight astern when the battle commenced. Sailing to the sound of the guns (and the flash of the firing), it caught up with the two combatants just as *Indefatigable* was preparing to renew the action. *Concorde* placed itself across *Virginie*'s stern, and waited. *Virginie*, unable to run, fired a gun to leeward, and set a light in its stern – a signal of surrender.

While *Virginie*'s surrender was due to the arrival of a fresh frigate, the battle had really been settled before then. *Indefatigable* was preparing to resume combat, and *Virginie* would have had little chance of success when that happened. *Virginie* had also taken significant casualties – 15 killed and 27 wounded in a crew of 339. *Indefatigable* had not lost one of its 327 men and officers.

AMBUSCADE vs BAÏONNAISE

The race did not always go to the swift and victory did not always go to the strong. One frigate duel that exemplified this point was the battle between HMS *Ambuscade* and MNF *Baïonnaise*, on 14 December 1798.

Ambuscade was a 32-gun 12-pdr frigate, elderly by the time of the battle. It had been launched in 1773, one of 17 medium frigates of the Amazon class built between 1771 and 1778. By 1798 it carried a main battery of 12-pdr long guns, with 24-pdr carronades

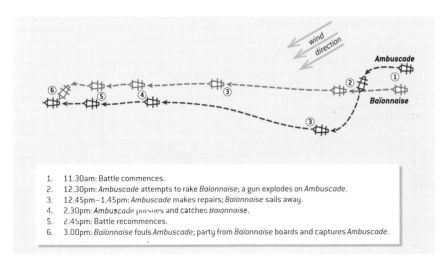

1.   11.30am: Battle commences.
2.   12.30pm: *Ambuscade* attempts to rake *Baïonnaise*; a gun explodes on *Ambuscade*.
3.   12.45pm–1.45pm: *Ambuscade* makes repairs; *Baïonnaise* sails away.
4.   2.30pm: *Ambuscade* pursues and catches *Baïonnaise*.
5.   2.45pm: Battle recommences.
6.   3.00pm: *Baïonnaise* fouls *Ambuscade*; party from *Baïonnaise* boards and captures *Ambuscade*.

This map shows the battle between HMS *Ambuscade* and MNF *Baïonnaise* on 14 December 1798. It traces the track of both ships and illustrates the major events during this frigate duel.

A Sea Service pistol. Used during boarding actions, these weapons were notoriously inaccurate at any range greater than 2yd, but were sturdy enough to be used as clubs after being fired. (Rama)

and 6-pdr long guns on its upper works, with a broadside weight of 270lb. In 1798 it formed part of the force blockading France's Biscayan coast. In December, the frigate had been on a successful cruise along the coast. It had captured three prizes earlier that month, but by 14 December *Ambuscade* was back on its blockade station off Bordeaux. Part of the crew was still off with prizes. Only 190 men of its 212-man complement were aboard on 14 December, and several of these – including its third lieutenant – were sick.

At 7.00am, in the pre-dawn twilight, *Ambuscade* spotted a sail to seaward. It raised no alarm, as the sail was expected to belong to HMS *Stag*, a 32-gun 18-pdr frigate, another ship of the Bordeaux blockade. Instead, it was *Baïonnaise*, returning from the West Indies to France.

Baïonnaise was a 28-gun ship, of a class originally rated as frigates by the *Marine nationale*, but by 1798 rated a corvette. It carried a main battery of French 8-pdrs, equivalent to the British 9-pdrs. With the brass *obusiers* and the 6-pdr long guns on its quarterdeck and forecastle, it threw a broadside of 156lb, only 60 per cent that of *Ambuscade*. It did carry a larger crew – 250 men, including its marines – and it had an additional 30 soldiers aboard, men returning from Cayenne.

Watch aboard *Baïonnaise* was even less alert than that on *Ambuscade*. Intent on reaching port after its transatlantic passage, it sailed directly towards *Ambuscade* for the next two hours, and was almost within gunshot before it reacted. Then, at 9.00am, realizing it was in the presence of a superior enemy ship, *Baïonnaise* hauled up into the wind, changed tack, added sail and made away from *Ambuscade*.

MNF *Baïonnaise* running foul of HMS *Ambuscade*, in an attempt to allow the French warship to board the British frigate. (AC)

Only at that point did Henry Jenkins, *Ambuscade*'s captain, realize the approaching ship was French, rather than the British *Stag*. He called up the watch below, ordered *Ambuscade* cleared for action, and set off in pursuit of the fleeing *Baïonnaise*.

It took 2 hours 30 minutes for *Ambuscade* to draw within gunshot of *Baïonnaise*. *Ambuscade* fired a shot in challenge. *Baïonnaise* fired once in response. Both ships hoisted their colours and shifted to battle sail.

The action commenced with an exchange of broadsides, and continued for an hour, the two ships sailing broadside to broadside, blazing away.

Then at 12.30pm, as *Ambuscade* dropped behind *Baïonnaise* to cross its stern and rake the French ship, one of *Ambuscade*'s waist 12-pdrs burst. The explosion destroyed the gangway, stove in the ship's boats stowed amidships on the booms and badly wounded 11 men – the crew of the burst gun and those of the two guns on either side of it. *Baïonnaise* used the confusion caused by *Ambuscade*'s burst gun to advantage. It made sail, and fled downwind.

Baïonnaise towing *Ambuscade* into port after its victory over the British frigate. Note the Tricolour flying over the White Ensign, a sign of victory. (AC)

Yet Captain Jenkins soon brought *Ambuscade* under control, made repairs and resumed his pursuit of *Baïonnaise*. This time, he was determined to catch *Baïonnaise*. Jenkins crowded on sail, and dropped to the lee side of the French warship to cut off escape. Passing along the previously disengaged side of *Baïonnaise*, *Ambuscade* resumed fire with its fresh starboard battery.

By this point *Baïonnaise* had suffered badly, sustaining heavy damage to its hull, injury to its rigging and spars and significant casualties among its crew. *Baïonnaise* was moving so slowly that *Ambuscade* shot ahead of *Baïonnaise* after resuming combat. By this point *Baïonnaise*'s captain and first lieutenant were both badly injured, and a junior lieutenant commanded the ship. Despite the damage done to *Ambuscade* by the explosion of its own 12-pdr, it was not nearly as badly damaged as *Baïonnaise*.

The officer commanding the troops carried by *Baïonnaise* then recommended boarding *Ambuscade* as the only means of successfully defeating the British. *Ambuscade* was now ahead of *Baïonnaise*, hauling in sail to bring *Baïonnaise* within its line of fire. The lieutenant commanding *Baïonnaise* ordered the helm put over, and *Baïonnaise*

OVERLEAF: MNF *BAÏONNAISE* CAPTURES HMS *AMBUSCADE*

The most improbable French victory of the wars against Britain occurred when MNF *Baïonnaise* took HMS *Ambuscade* through boarding. While *Baïonnaise* had a smaller broadside than *Ambuscade*, it had a much larger crew, one augmented by the 30 soldiers the small frigate had brought from Cayenne. Nevertheless, *Baïonnaise*'s musketry and gunnery made a significant contribution to its victory. By the time *Baïonnaise*'s crew boarded, every officer aboard *Ambuscade* was dead or injured, including its captain, all of its lieutenants and the master. Command of *Ambuscade* had devolved on the purser, a warrant officer whose major responsibility was logistical, keeping the ship victualled.

As shown overleaf, the boarding action occurred after *Baïonnaise* rammed *Ambuscade* in the after quarter. The collision knocked down *Ambuscade*'s after bulwarks and the mizzen chains, uprooting the shrouds holding *Ambuscade*'s mizzen mast upright. The mast collapsed after being struck by *Baïonnaise*'s bowsprit, which also unshipped *Ambuscade*'s wheel. The bowsprit collapsed across *Ambuscade*'s quarterdeck, almost depopulated by earlier fire from *Baïonnaise*.

Baïonnaise's crew used the bowsprit as a bridge, soldiers, sailors and marines swarming across it and over *Ambuscade*'s sides to swamp the few defenders, including the purser, on *Ambuscade*'s quarterdeck. With the afterguard quickly overwhelmed, the French gained control of *Ambuscade*'s upper works, and forced the crew still alive on the gun deck and below to surrender.

struck *Ambuscade*'s starboard quarterdeck bulwark. The collision brought down *Ambuscade*'s mizzen mast, and destroyed its wheel.

Ambuscade slipped forward until *Baïonnaise*'s anchor fluke dug into *Ambuscade*'s starboard rudder chain, locking the two ships together. *Baïonnaise*'s bow was firmly fixed on *Ambuscade*'s quarter gallery, *Baïonnaise*'s bowsprit lying across *Ambuscade*'s quarterdeck. Neither ship's guns could bear on the other ship. The battle devolved to a musketry exchange – one in which *Baïonnaise*'s superior numbers of men soon told.

Assisted by swivel guns on its forecastle, *Baïonnaise*'s crew soon dominated *Ambuscade*'s quarterdeck. *Ambuscade*'s marines were soon swept clear by marksmen from *Baïonnaise*. So were *Ambuscade*'s officers. The master, captain, all of its lieutenants and the lieutenant of marines were either killed or seriously wounded. William Murray, *Ambuscade*'s purser, was called to the quarterdeck to take command.

Shortly after Murray took command, the gunner reported to him that *Ambuscade* was on fire aft. Several spare powder cartridges in the aft gun deck had caught fire when sparks from a fired gun touched them off. The flash-over of gunpowder severely burned the crew of the aftermost gun. It also created a panic among the rest of the crew on the gun deck, who fled forwards, believing the magazine was on fire.

As Murray attempted to rally the crew, the French boarded the almost-abandoned quarterdeck. Using *Baïonnaise*'s bowsprit as a gangway, sailors, marines and soldiers swarmed over *Baïonnaise*'s forecastle onto *Ambuscade*'s quarterdeck. *Ambuscade*'s crew resisted – among the French dead was the officer commanding the troops aboard *Baïonnaise*, killed during the boarding action – but the weight of numbers told. The French soon commanded *Ambuscade*'s quarterdeck, then its upper works. Trapped below, *Ambuscade*'s remaining crew surrendered.

The butcher's bill was heavy on both sides. *Ambuscade* lost ten killed and 36 seriously wounded, including every commissioned officer aboard. *Baïonnaise* had suffered 60 casualties – 30 dead and 30 seriously wounded. Even so, the French were victorious, in the only ship-to-ship action over the entire period of the French Revolutionary and Napoleonic Wars won by an inferior French warship.

SYBILLE vs *FORTE*

While *Baïonnaise*'s fight represented a unique instance when a French warship defeated a larger British warship, Royal Navy captains were expected to fight – and best – *Marine nationale* opponents larger than their own ships. Such victories happened less often in reality than on the pages of nautical fiction novels, and usually involved special factors that overturned the simple balance of broadside weight. Yet on at least one occasion – the battle between HMS *Sybille* and MNF *Forte* – a weaker British frigate outgunned and captured a significantly superior French counterpart.

Forte was one of the French experiments with a 24-pdr frigate. Launched in 1795, in 1798 it was at Île de France, now Mauritius. Late that year it was sent from Île de France for a cruise against British merchant shipping in the Bay of Bengal. By February its actions had attracted the attention of the Royal Navy in India, and *Sybille* was sent in search of *Forte*.

Sybille was a French prize, a 40-gun 18-pdr frigate of the Hébé class. Captured by the 50-gun two-decker HMS *Romney* in 1794, it was subsequently refitted as a standard 38-gun 18-pdr Royal Navy frigate. Captain Edward Cook, commanding *Sybille*, was seeking *Forte* near the mouth of the Bengal River. At 8.30pm on 27 February 1799, well after sunset, flashes were seen to the north-west, which continued for the next 30 minutes. At first, Cook assumed the flashes were lightning. As they continued, he began to suspect they were gunfire and sailed towards them, extinguishing the lights on *Sybille*. At 9.30pm his perseverance was rewarded. Three ships were spotted clustered together south-east of *Sybille*.

The ships were *Forte* and two merchant prizes, *Endeavour* and *Lord Mornington*, whose capture was the cause of the flashes seen earlier. *Sybille* and *Forte* had sailed past each other in the dark. Suspecting one of the unidentified ships to be *Forte*, Cook continued sailing on his current course to get upwind of the ships and gain the weather gage, which took *Sybille* another half-hour to achieve. At 10.00pm *Sybille* put about, and doubled back towards the three ships, now two miles downwind of it. The wind was light, and it was midnight by the time *Sybille* drew within a mile of the three ships and set its course on the biggest of the three – *Forte*.

By this time *Sybille* had switched to battle sail – topsails, jibs and spanker. As *Sybille* approached, *Forte* turned to starboard, exposing its broadside, and began firing its guns individually, firing seven shots and bringing down *Sybille*'s jib. *Forte*'s captain, Beaulieu-Leloup, had concluded that the approaching ship was another East Indiaman, and was apparently determined to capture it with as little damage as possible. *Sybille*'s initial refusal to return fire compounded the illusion.

Cook was reserving *Sybille*'s fire until he could use it to best effect. The initial broadside in a ship-to-ship battle was the only one that was carefully loaded and aimed. Once the battle commenced, subsequent shots were loaded and fired as quickly as possible by the crews, trading rate-of-fire for deliberation. In this case, *Forte*'s turn, intended to expose its broadside to *Sybille*, also exposed *Forte*'s stern to *Sybille*.

Cook seized the opportunity; sailing *Sybille* directly behind *Forte*'s stern, so close that *Forte*'s spanker boom hung over *Sybille*. From that distance, *Sybille*'s broadside was deadly. As *Forte*'s stern passed into the field of each of *Sybille*'s broadside guns, each gun fired, sending a cannonball – 32, 18 or 9lb of iron – down the length of *Forte*'s gun decks. Once past *Forte*, *Sybille* wore around, turning 180 degrees, again passing *Forte*'s stern, and firing another raking broadside down the length of the French frigate with *Sybille*'s previously unengaged battery.

Sybille's initial broadside created sufficient confusion aboard *Forte* that *Sybille*'s turn went unnoticed. *Forte* began to fire its larboard battery at the nearest ship that was observed – which happened to be one of its prizes, confused for *Sybille* in the moonless darkness. It was not until *Sybille* raked *Forte* a second time and ranged up on *Forte*'s starboard side that *Sybille*'s true position was realized. *Forte*'s crew manned its starboard guns and the two ships began exchanging broadsides.

Launched at Toulon in 1799, MNF *Egyptienne* was a sister ship to *Forte*. Like *Forte*, *Égyptienne* was captured by the Royal Navy. it served as a frigate in the Royal Navy for eight years. (AC)

Forte's captain was hunting East Indiamen, such as this one, *Earl of Balcarras*. With cargoes from China or India, they were rich prizes. (AC)

For the next 90 minutes, both ships blazed away at each other. The range separating the two ships was never more than 25yd and was frequently closer. Both captains were mortally wounded within ten minutes of each other: Cook at 1.30am and Beaulieu-Leloup at 1.40am. *Forte*'s first lieutenant was killed soon afterwards. *Sybille* fired low, into *Forte*'s hull, while *Forte*'s gunners fired high, and the results were predictable. *Sybille* was damaged aloft, while *Forte* took its damage in the hull. By 2.00am *Forte*'s fire was slackening. At 2.30am, with only four guns still in action, *Forte*'s senior surviving lieutenant ceased firing, sending the surviving crew to loose *Forte*'s topgallant sails, and flee the *Sybille*. This was an all-hands operation by this time, as *Sybille*'s fire had damaged *Forte*'s lower masts.

When *Forte* ceased firing, *Sybille* also ceased firing. The two ships were within hail, and *Sybille* asked *Forte* if it had surrendered. Receiving no answer to the hail, despite hearing conversations in French, *Sybille* resumed firing on *Forte*. Receiving no return fire, *Sybille* again ceased firing. When *Forte*'s crew began taking to the rigging, *Sybille*'s first lieutenant, Lucius Hardyman, now in command, realized the French frigate was trying to escape. Despite the damage to *Sybille*'s rigging, he ordered *Sybille*'s fore course and topgallants set. He also resumed firing at *Forte*. The renewed fire brought down *Forte*'s mizzen mast, soon followed by the main mast, fore mast and bowsprit. Completely dismasted, *Forte* was a drifting wreck.

Sybille was not in much better shape. Most of its standing and running rigging had been cut away by *Forte*'s fire. Hardyman anchored *Sybille* in 17 fathoms to conduct repairs, as *Forte* could wait until the lines had been replaced. As *Sybille* spliced lines, *Forte* drifted closer. Finally a voice aboard *Forte*, in English, called for *Sybille* to send a boat over. It was one of the British prisoners aboard *Forte*. Communication finally established between the two ships, *Forte*'s senior surviving lieutenant could no longer play for time to escape. He surrendered *Forte*.

STATISTICS AND ANALYSIS

Of the 45 frigate duels fought between British and French frigates between 1793 and 1814, 35 were won by the Royal Navy, seven were inconclusive, and only three were won by the *Marine nationale*. Of the 38 victories, 35, including three French victories, resulted in the capture of the enemy ship. (In the other three the losing frigate – French in each case – avoided capture due to the arrival of friendly reinforcements before the victor could take possession.) These statistics reveal an overwhelming British superiority in single-ship combat. A *Marine nationale* frigate encountering a Royal Navy frigate could expect to avoid capture in only one out of every five battles and win fewer than seven per cent of these encounters. What factors contributed to this disparity?

Note that for the purposes of this discussion, only single-ship actions have been examined. This is defined as an action fought between two frigates with no other warship within sight at the start of the battle, and where other warships appeared only after the battle was decided – even if the losing frigate surrendered to the new arrival. An example of the latter is the battle fought between *Indefatigable* and *Virginie*. Although two other British frigates were present at the start of the chase, by the time combat began both *Amazon* and *Concorde* were out of sight – hours away from the two combatants. The battle had been decided before their reappearance. *Virginie* could not have escaped from *Indefatigable*; Pellew had temporarily disengaged to repair his own rigging (so *Indefatigable* could attack *Virginie* without being fired at), and would have taken *Virginie* unassisted had *Amazon* and *Concorde* not appeared.

Nearly a quarter of frigate duels ended this way – with one frigate battered into submission, to be captured or to escape when other ships appeared. Nearly all frigate

The wounded in a frigate battle were taken down to the cockpit, as shown here, to be treated by the ship's surgeon. The dead were left on deck or tossed overboard. Casualties in the battle between *Sybille* and *Forte* were brutal. *Forte* had 80 wounded. (OC)

duels occurred where other warships were likely to be present. Despite the vast size of the seas, the places where ships are likely to be found are much smaller: headlands, straits, narrows and approaches to major seaports. Ships attacking enemy commerce – British or French – frequented those locations in search of merchant prizes. British warships would either patrol nautical landmarks seeking French commerce raiders, or cruise off French ports to blockade them.

A battle fought in such locations had a significant chance of drawing additional participants. Three-quarters of all frigate duels were fought in just two areas. The majority, 21, were fought in the western approaches to Britain – including the Bay of Biscay and western English Channel. Four of these started near Ushant, four close to the French naval port of Rochefort and four within a few hours' sail of the Channel Islands. Eight other frigate duels were fought in the Caribbean, including four fought within sight of the island of Guadeloupe.

How did the origins of the frigate used affect victory? All French victories were won by French-built frigates against British-built frigates. All the British victories were won against frigates built in French shipyards. While the *Marine nationale* had taken several Royal Navy frigates as prizes during the American Revolutionary Wars, and had used these ships as frigates during that earlier conflict, none of them was employed as a cruiser after the French Revolution. However, 11 British victories were won by French-built frigates fighting under the British flag, and one by a frigate originally built for the Spanish Navy.

Napoleon has been variously quoted as stating that God was on the side of either the best artillery or the bigger battalions. The table below shows that the first aphorism was more correct than the second. The frigate with the heavier broadside won nearly half of the frigate duels fought to victory, while the frigate possessing a larger crew was victorious in only a quarter of the clashes.

The French sugar island of Guadeloupe served as a magnet for warships of both Britain and France. No fewer than four frigate duels were fought in its vicinity. (AC)

Gunnery and crew superiority's roles in victory

	Winning frigate	British victory	French victory
Superior broadside	18	16	2
Inferior broadside	10	9	1
Broadside parity	10	10	0
Larger crew	8	5	3
Smaller crew	22	22	0
Equal crews	8	8	0

More revealing is the difference that the victor's nationality made. The Royal Navy won virtually every battle in which it was superior in weight of broadside. (The sole loss was that of *Ambuscade* to *Baïonnaise*.) They also won every battle with parity in broadside weight or crew (parity in broadside or crew is defined as a difference less than ten per cent that of the opposing ship) and eight of the ten battles fought in which they were inferior in broadside to the French. By contrast, the *Marine nationale* regularly lost to the Royal Navy even when *Marine nationale* frigates had a heavier broadside or larger crew. Of the two French victories over inferior Royal Navy frigates, in one the French broadside was 250 per cent larger than the British frigate. In both duels other French frigates were close at hand. While they did not take part in the fighting, they prevented the escape of the British ship.

While weight of metal was important, 'better artillery' was also a function of accuracy and rate of fire. A Royal Navy gun crew was expected to be able to fire two shots every three minutes. Most frigates had a corps of experienced sailors who could serve as gun captains; while lacking formal training, these men had practical experience in firing a gun. With relatively little live-fire practice conducted aboard its ships, however, Royal Navy gunnery was not terribly accurate. Usually, less than ten per cent

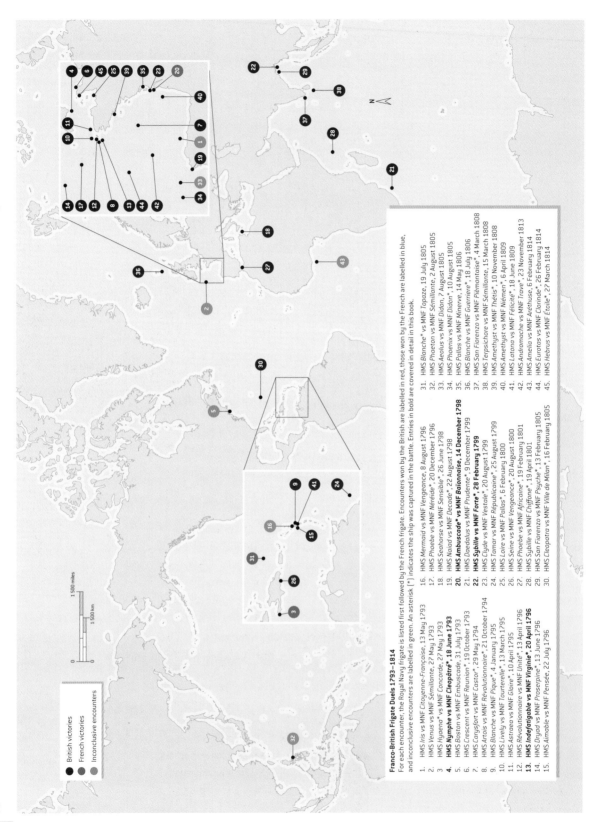

Franco-British Frigate Duels 1793–1814

For each encounter, the Royal Navy frigate is listed first followed by the French frigate. Encounters won by the British are labelled in red, those won by the French are labelled in blue, and inconclusive encounters are labelled in green. An asterisk (*) indicates the ship was captured in the battle. Entries in bold are covered in detail in this book.

1. HMS *Iris* vs MNF *Citoyenne-Française*, 13 May 1793
2. HMS *Venus* vs MNF *Sémillante*, 27 May 1793
3. HMS *Hyæna** vs MNF *Concorde*, 27 May 1793
4. **HMS *Nymphe* vs MNF *Cleopâtre**, 18 June 1793**
5. HMS *Boston* vs MNF *Embuscade*, 31 July 1793
6. HMS *Crescent* vs MNF *Réunion**, 19 October 1793
7. HMS *Carysfort* vs MNF *Castor**, 29 May 1794
8. HMS *Artois* vs MNF *Révolutionnaire**, 21 October 1794
9. HMS *Blanche* vs MNF *Pique**, 4 January 1795
10. HMS *Lively* vs MNF *Tourterelle**, 13 March 1795
11. HMS *Astraea* vs MNF *Gloire**, 10 April 1795
12. HMS *Révolutionnaire* vs MNF *Unité**, 13 April 1796
13. **HMS *Indefatigable* vs MNF *Virginie**, 20 April 1796**
14. HMS *Dryad* vs MNF *Proserpine**, 13 June 1796
15. HMS *Aimable* vs MNF *Pensée*, 22 July 1796
16. HMS *Mermaid* vs MNF *Vengeance*, 8 August 1796
17. HMS *Phoebe* vs MNF *Néréide**, 20 December 1796
18. HMS *Seahorse* vs MNF *Sensible**, 26 June 1798
19. HMS *Naiad* vs MNF *Decade**, 22 August 1798
20. **HMS *Ambuscade** vs MNF *Baïonnaise*, 14 December 1798**
21. HMS *Daedalus* vs MNF *Prudente**, 9 December 1799
22. **HMS *Sybille* vs MNF *Forte**, 28 February 1799**
23. HMS *Clyde* vs MNF *Vestale**, 20 August 1799
24. HMS *Tamar* vs MNF *Republicaine**, 25 August 1799
25. HMS *Loire* vs MNF *Pallas**, 6 February 1800
26. HMS *Seine* vs MNF *Vengeance**, 20 August 1800
27. HMS *Phoebe* vs MNF *Africaine**, 19 February 1801
28. **HMS *Sybille* vs MNF *Chiffone**, 19 April 1801**
29. HMS *San Fiorenzo* vs MNF *Psyche**, 13 February 1805
30. HMS *Cleopatra* vs MNF *Ville de Milan**, 16 February 1805
31. HMS *Blanche** vs MNF *Topaze*, 19 July 1805
32. HMS *Phaeton* vs MNF *Sémillante*, 2 August 1805
33. HMS *Aeolus* vs MNF *Didon*, 7 August 1805
34. HMS *Phoenix* vs MNF *Didon**, 10 August 1805
35. HMS *Pallas* vs MNF *Minerve*, 14 May 1806
36. HMS *Blanche* vs MNF *Guerriere**, 18 July 1806
37. HMS *San Fiorenzo* vs MNF *Piémontaise**, 4 March 1808
38. HMS *Terpsichore* vs MNF *Sémillante*, 15 March 1808
39. HMS *Amethyst* vs MNF *Thetis**, 10 November 1808
40. HMS *Amethyst* vs MNF *Niémen**, 6 April 1809
41. HMS *Latona* vs MNF *Félicité**, 18 June 1809
42. HMS *Andromache* vs MNF *Trave**, 23 November 1813
43. HMS *Amelia* vs MNF *Aréthuse*, 6 February 1814
44. HMS *Eurotas* vs MNF *Clorinde**, 26 February 1814
45. HMS *Hebrus* vs MNF *Étoile**, 27 March 1814

British victories
French victories
Inconclusive encounters

0   1 500 miles

0   1 500 km

of all shots fired by British guns found their mark, even though the preferred range was 50yd or less.

The abolition of the *Corps de Cannoniers-Matelots* in 1792 robbed the *Marine nationale* of experienced gunners. Even after it was reconstituted, the replacement gunners lacked the experience of their predecessors, and – due to the British blockade – had relatively little opportunity to hone their skills. As a result French gunnery was generally mediocre, even by the standards of the day. The rate of fire was often half that of the Royal Navy, and its accuracy less than half that of the British. With double the rate of fire and double the accuracy of their opponents, even a British frigate with an inferior battery could hold its own – and often win – against a larger French foe.

Crew size usually proved less important. Royal Navy frigates twice defeated *Marine nationale* frigates with crews nearly three times as large as their own. The raw numbers of men aboard a frigate was less important than the composition of the crew. The smaller Royal Navy crews had a greater proportion of sailors than a comparable or even larger *Marine nationale* vessel, and this superiority in seamanship allowed Royal Navy frigates to outsail and outmanoeuvre their French opponents. This quality allowed *Indefatigable* to catch *Virginie*, and allowed *Sybille* to twice rake *Forte*, and then attack *Forte* from an unexpected direction. Similarly, the greater seamanship of British crews allowed *Sybille*'s men to rapidly repair the ship, and capture the still-dismasted *Forte*.

HMS *Seine* started its career in the *Marine nationale*. After its capture and incorporation into the Royal Navy it won one of the 12 frigate duels won by foreign-built Royal Navy frigates against the *Marine nationale*. (AC)

Boarding actions were generally successful only if the command structure of the attacked frigate had already collapsed and it could not organize an effective defence. (AC)

Often the difference in crew size was due to the addition of soldiers to a French vessel to augment the frigate's marine contingent, with the idea that they could tip the scales during a boarding action. These men were armed with muskets and were to be used as marksmen. Unless the two ships were separated by less than 30yd, musketry was ineffective, however. The only case where a French frigate overwhelmed a British frigate with musketry and boarding was the battle between *Baïonnaise* and *Ambuscade*, when the British allowed the French vessel to foul *Ambuscade*. This allowed the French superiority in musketry to clear the British quarterdeck of most of the crew there prior to the boarding.

While many frigate duels concluded with a boarding action, the decision to board ratified victory rather than deciding the battle. Only 11 members of *Nymphe*'s crew boarded *Cléopâtre*, yet once they controlled the quarterdeck the nearly 260 uninjured members of *Cléopâtre*'s crew meekly surrendered. Similarly, by the time *Baïonnaise*'s crew boarded *Ambuscade* only a handful of British were still on the quarterdeck, and most of its officers were casualties.

To succeed, a boarding action required a collapse of the command structure of the boarded frigate. By the time Pellew ordered *Cléopâtre* boarded, *Cléopâtre*'s captain and all three of its lieutenants were injured. The senior surviving officer aboard *Ambuscade* when it was boarded was the purser – a warrant officer junior to every commissioned officer and virtually every other warrant officer on a ship. Other battles concluded by boarding showed a similar pattern: a command structure in disorder, unable to mount an organized resistance to the boarding attempt.

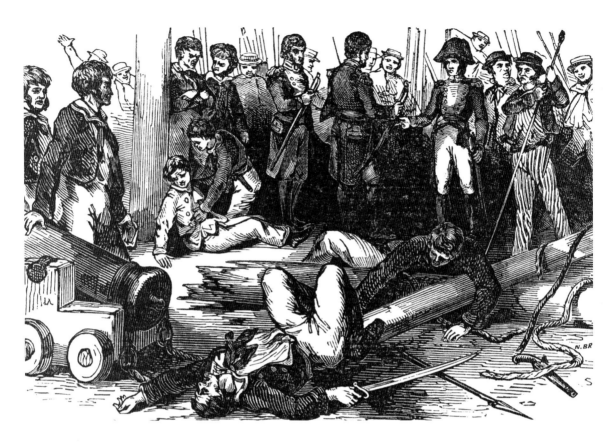

A frigate duel was a dangerous occasion for a frigate captain and his first lieutenant. In three of the four battles discussed at least one of the two captains was killed or seriously wounded in combat. In two, both captains and their first lieutenants became casualties. These ratios hold for all frigate duels – in the vast majority of them at least one captain became a casualty. Both the captain and first lieutenant were stationed at the quarterdeck, the most exposed part of the ship, and commissioned officers also wore distinctive uniforms which visibly marked them as leaders. Eliminating enemy leaders was the quickest way to win a battle, as it caused the collapse of the command structure. Most sailors and marines were more concerned with ending a battle quickly than they were with the glory of taking a rival commander captive.

All of these factors together explain the disproportionate level of British success. British ships were generally better armed than their French counterparts. Their crews were better-trained and more experienced in working as a team. Their officers were more experienced, and a Royal Navy frigate crew generally had better depth of experience in its officer corps than did its *Marine nationale* counterpart. The French fought bravely and competently – just not as well as the British. In battle, being second best means losing.

This romanticized depiction of a surrender, with the defeated captain presenting his sword to the victor, rarely happened, as only a small fraction of frigate duels ended with both captains uninjured. Sometimes both captains and both first lieutenants became casualties. (AC)

CONCLUSION

On 26 March 1814, the *Marine nationale* frigates *Étoile* and *Sultane* were returning to France after a cruise to the Cape Verde Islands when the pair was spotted by three Royal Navy warships patrolling the English Channel. The French frigates split up. *Sultane* would be run down by the 74-gun *Hannibal* and the 16-gun brig sloop *Sparrow*. The 44-gun *Étoile* was left to HMS *Hebrus*, a 38-gun 18-pdr Scamander-class frigate built of yellow pine as part of an emergency shipbuilding programme prompted by the War of 1812. A day-long chase followed, with *Étoile* attempting to escape by slipping through the rock-lined Race of Alderney. *Hebrus* finally caught its quarry at 2.00am the next day, battering *Étoile* into submission in a two-hour fight.

This proved to be the last single-ship frigate action of the Napoleonic Wars. The *Marine nationale* played no significant role in the Hundred Days campaign of 1815, triggered by Napoleon's return from exile. There was not time enough to prepare ships for sea before Napoleon's defeat at Waterloo ended that war. *Hebrus*'s capture of *Étoile* may well have also been the last single-ship action fought between two sailing frigates.

The sailing warship's day was passing. Even then the United States had the steam battery *Demilogos* under construction in New York Harbor. Sail would dominate until the 1840s, when screw propulsion replaced vulnerable paddlewheels, making steam power practical in combat. The wooden warship would last two decades longer, until wood was doomed by the appearance of the iron-hulled HMS *Warrior* in 1859.

The sailing frigates and frigate captains of 1793–1814 dwindled away over the next four decades. Death overtook the captains, and the breaker's yard got most of the frigates. Today only one warship that served during those wars in the Royal Navy or *Marine nationale* still exists, the three-deck ship-of-the-line HMS *Victory*. Two Royal Navy sailing frigates whose design dates to the Napoleonic era still exist – HMS *Trincomalee* (now a museum ship in Hartlepool) and HMS *Unicorn* (a museum ship in Dundee).

Both are Leda-class frigates, a classic 18-pdr frigate design of the war, but both were launched after 1815. A few modern replicas exist, including HMS *Rose* (renamed *Surprise* in 2003) and the *Marine nationale*'s *Hermione*. Regardless, these are the last examples of the types of frigates that paired off between the Royal Navy and *Marine nationale*.

In 1828, a Royal Navy captain, bored by peacetime service, wrote a novel to pass the time. The captain had served as a midshipman under Cochrane aboard the 38-gun frigate *Imperieuse* in 1811. In 1812 he joined the 32-gun *Aeolis*, then serving on the North American station, winning promotion to lieutenant. He drew on his experiences to write a book about wartime service aboard a Royal Navy frigate, *The Naval Officer or Scenes in the Life and Adventures of Frank Mildmay*, published in 1829.

The book was a commercial success, and the captain, Frederick Marryat, soon had a new career as a novelist. His adventure tales, including his best-known book, *Mr. Midshipman Easy*, created a new literary genre – the nautical adventure. He would be imitated by a long line of successors, including C.S. Forester, whose Horatio Hornblower stories popularized the serial novel, and Patrick O'Brian, who took the concept to a literary apogee with his series on Jack Aubrey and Stephen Maturin. In the process they have kept interest in the frigate duel alive.

Although ordered and completed after the Napoleonic Wars, HMS *Unicorn* was built to a modified Leda-class design – the most numerous class of frigates constructed by the Royal Navy during the French Revolutionary and Napoleonic Wars. On completion, *Unicorn* was immediately roofed over and placed in ordinary, and so is the best-preserved of surviving frigates from the age of sail. (Eddie Dowds)

FURTHER READING

The most comprehensive account of the frigate battles between the *Marine nationale* and the Royal Navy is one of the earliest – the six-volume *The Naval History of Great Britain from the Declaration of War by France in 1793 to the Accession of King George IV* by William James. James gives balanced accounts of battles, with less chest-thumping than normally encountered. I obtained a set of the 1859 volumes (it was originally published in 1822–24) in the 1980s, which I relied upon heavily in writing this book. Another major source was William Laird Clowes' *The Royal Navy, A History from the Earliest Times to the Present* (Sampson, Lowes, Marston & Co., London, 1897–1901), with volumes 4 and 5 covering the period of interest.

Information on the frigates and their design was extracted from Robert Gardiner's three books: *The First Frigates: Nine Pounder And Twelve Pounder Frigates 1748–1815* (Conway, London, 1992), *The Heavy Frigate: Eighteen-Pounder Frigates 1778–1800* (Conway, London, 1994) and *Frigates of the Napoleonic Wars* (Chatham, London, 2000).

The social history of both the Royal Navy and the *Marine nationale*, general information on shipbuilding practices, administration and the strategic situation was extracted from Clowes and the writings of N.A.M. Rodger, especially *Command of the Ocean: A Naval History of Britain 1649–1815* (W.W. Norton & Co., New York, NY and London, 2004) and E.H. Jenkins's *A History of the French Navy From its Beginnings to the Present* (MacDonald & Jane's, London, 1973).

Gunnery information came from Spencer Tucker's *Arming the Fleet: U.S. Navy Ordnance in the Muzzle-Loading Era* (Naval Institute Press, Annapolis, MD, 1989) and Douglas Howard's *A Treatise on Naval Gunnery, 2nd Edition* (John Murray, London, 1829).

Two sources on the timber issue were Robert G. Albion's *Forests and Sea Power: The Timber Problem of the Royal Navy, 1652–1862* (Archon Books, Hamden, CT, 1965)

and *Forests and French Sea Power, 1660–1789* (University of Toronto Press, Toronto, 1956) by Paul W. Bamford.

Two 19th-century French sources were used: Eugéne Pacini's *La Marine: Arsenaux, Navires, Équipages, Navigation, Atterranges, Combats* (L. Curmer, Paris, 1844) and *Histoire Nationale de la Marine et des Marins Français* (Librairie Illustrée, Paris, 1880) by Jules Trousset.

Most of the 19th-century sources can be found online at or at Google Books (books.google.com). Numerous other sources were used, but space precludes listing them. One online site that may interest aficionados of the sailing era is 'Three Decks – Warships in the Age of Sail' (threedecks.org). While not a final authority, it has much of interest.

More fictional frigate duels have been fought in 20th- and 21st-century novels than were ever fought between British and French frigates during the French Revolutionary and Napoleonic Wars. Many can be found on public library bookshelves. Besides C.S. Forester's and Patrick O'Brian's books, examples include Alexander Kent's Richard Bolitho saga, Dudley Pope's Nicholas Ramage novels, and C. Northcote Parkinson's Richard Delancy collection. In all these books, the heroes spent time commanding fictional sailing frigates in the Royal Navy during the Great Age of Sail. Some are more accurate than others; Pope and Parkinson were naval historians. My personal favourite is one written by Dewey Lambdin, centred on a Royal Navy officer, Alan Lewrie. Although an American author, Lambdin captures the period accurately and in an entertaining manner.

Having served as a midshipman under Lord Cochrane, Frederick Marryat went on to command the frigate HMS *Ariadne*, a model of which, built under Marryat's supervision, is shown here. It was a frigate similar to *Imperieuse*, the frigate on which he had served under Cochrane's command. [AC]

INDEX

References to illustrations and plates are shown in **bold**.